Guidance
from
The Therapist Parent

This book offers explanations, proven strategies,
and playful activities that children respond to.

Planetary Press and Publishing Pty Ltd
Fennell Bay, NSW, 2283 Australia

First published by Planetary Press and Publishing 2023
Copyright © Krysten Taprell - The Therapist Parent

Cover design and Illustrations© Natalie Herington 2023
Natalie Herington -Bird Valley Illustration & Design
Artwork Illustrations © Krysten Taprell 2023
Krysten Taprell - The Therapist Parent
Printed in Australia

ISBN: 978-0-6459044-0-6 (Soft Cover)
ISBN: 978-0-6459044-1-3 (EBook)

A catalogue record is available from the
National Library of Australia

www.planetarypp.com.au

Dedication

I want to dedicate this book to every child I have ever worked with, cared for or has been in my life. You are my greatest teachers and the ones who caused me to change my thinking and develop myself. I am still inspired every day to continue learning more because of the influence of these beautiful children.

I also want to acknowledge my husband and children for taking this journey with me. Your support and acceptance of me through the crazy life we lead is truly appreciated. Who knows where life will take us next? As long as we do it together, I'm in. Love you always and forever.

About the Author

Krysten is a psychologist who has worked with children and families for over 20 years. She has extensive experience working with people with Autism, including being involved in diagnostic testing.

Having worked within schools, private practices, and government agencies in rural Australia, Krysten felt that the long waiting lists and lack of services often left parents without information and ideas to help their children. In response, she has created a range of innovative methods, advice, a children's book, and therapeutic toys to help bring proven strategies to fill this gap. These are featured on her website and shared via her social media channels. This book conveniently compiles this guidance and Krysten's proven techniques in an immediately practical package, ready for parents to apply to their child's needs.

What I Have Learned

I want to lay all my cards on the table and be completely transparent. I don't profess to be a 'parenting expert.' What I am is experienced. I have had good and bad experiences. I have learned great things, but I have also made great mistakes, which I have also learned from.

I became a psychologist in the year 2000. As with everything in the last twenty-odd years, there have been a lot of changes to psychological practice. Early on, I embraced conventional 'wisdom,' emphasising firmness, consistency, and consequences. We were very rules-based, with lots of time-outs and 'thinking chairs' for behaviour modification. The Supernanny became a big hit with her 'naughty spot.' However, it wasn't until I became a parent myself that I truly grasped the complexities of raising children.

Early in our marriage, my husband became involved in caring for children. I foolishly believed that this and my experience as a young psychologist would have prepared us for having our own family. How wrong I was! I had a lot of theory-based knowledge but no practical experience of what trauma-induced behaviour looked like.

I had seen children in my office for years but never in my home, which had always been a safe place away from work. Parenting is simple in an office when you only have to see that child for an hour a fortnight. Parenting when you have been up four times in the night, driven children to all their activities, tried to manage kids fighting and meltdowns, washed mountains of laundry, and still gone to work is hard! The real-world challenges of parenting reshaped my perspective.

There are so many things I would do differently if I had my time again.

In retrospect, I've come to understand that strict reward and punishment methods yield limited results. This parenting style just doesn't work holistically. If I could take away all the times we punished these kids for the behaviours we experienced, I would in a heartbeat. Making a kid feel worse by punishing them for their behaviour simply doesn't work. It often exacerbates the issue. Let's face it: nobody will improve their behaviour if they constantly feel 'in trouble.'

We were taught to give consequence after consequence and believed we were doing the 'right' thing. However, this approach strained our relationships and blurred the lines between discipline and punishment. Now we understand that discipline guides and directs, while punishment only damages a child's view of themselves. I now know that you can't expect positive change with a child if there is no connection in the relationship, and I appreciate that nurturing a caring, empathetic bond with a child is paramount.

So, Here Is What I Have Learned:

Connection Is Key: While 'connected parenting' or 'gentle parenting' has gained attention today, it was often overlooked in the past. We understood the importance of mother-baby attachment but didn't delve into the parent-child connection beyond infancy.

In essence, connection means fostering a caring, trusting, and empathetic relationship, which can be challenging. Recognising that children use behaviour to express needs, even if not in ways adults prefer, is vital. Empathising with children and addressing their needs strengthens the parent-child bond.

Our expectations of children often exceed those we have for ourselves. Imagine working in an environment where you constantly feel in trouble, isolated (in time-out), and unheard — would you stay or feel motivated to improve? Instead of punishment, fostering a genuine connection motivates children to listen and grow rather than feel shame or fear.

Communicate on Their Level: While we recognise developmental milestones like crawling, walking, and talking, we often overlook the development of communication skills. Communication involves not just words but also expressing thoughts and feelings and understanding others' emotions. It's unrealistic to expect children to excel at this.

When children react emotionally to being told "No," I often hear parents say, "That behaviour is not appropriate." To a three-year-old! Children of this age are not able to understand 'appropriate behaviour,' nor that their behaviour can be controlled. Their reactions are an instinctive way to communicate a feeling. We need to meet our children where they are developmentally and emotionally.

We sometimes forget that children are individuals with feelings, thoughts, and beliefs. Limited language proficiency doesn't mean they can't express themselves. We just need to help them communicate in a way they are capable of. Listening and discussing emotions when everyone is calm can reveal surprising insights into a child's feelings and needs. Nobody can think clearly when they are upset.

Discipline Is Not Punishment: People are now starting to understand that there is a difference, but for so long, the belief was that people needed to be punished to learn. True discipline is instruction, teaching, and guiding. Punishment, on the other hand, means to inflict a penalty, pain, or loss. We don't have to make our kids hurt and feel upset to make them learn. We do have to teach and explain.

Now, this doesn't mean that they get away with everything. We still have limits and rules of what is okay, but our priority is to teach, not harm. We work with the child on what has happened and why. It is also essential that we ask our children what they think they should do to 'fix' a problem and what they might do next time. By talking about these and how other people might feel, we empower them to build problem-solving skills and empathy.

Practise Kindness (to Your Child and Yourself): We're all doing our best, both parents and children. Children rarely intend to annoy or upset us on purpose; they understand that everyone benefits when their parents are happy. Parents make mistakes, too, and we must approach our children and ourselves with kindness.

I advocate for 'positive/gentle parenting' because I've learned it's the best and most effective approach, albeit through difficult experiences. Sharing this knowledge, I'm saddened I didn't learn these lessons sooner. My hope is that others can learn from them without enduring the same hardships.

Foreword

Every once in a while, a book comes along that I want to gift every parent. This is one of those rare books. Krysten has written an informative, easy-to-read, hands-on guide for anyone who wants to understand the children in their lives better. More than that, she wants to support us to become the competent, compassionate caregivers we long to be.

Krysten and I serendipitously crossed paths in cyberspace. Physically, we're an ocean apart as I'm in Canada and she lives in Australia, but we instantly became virtual friends. We share the intention of wanting to make parenting more joyful for parents by offering insight into what moves children to behave in the ways they do. We've both dedicated ourselves to trying to make the complex and sometimes overwhelming topic of child development simpler by putting it into everyday language. When we strip away what might be rather intimidating academic terminology, we're left with the core message. These kernels of insight can help us to make sense of common and frequently misunderstood behaviours in children.

Parenting in the fast-paced digital world means we literally have an information superhighway at our fingertips day and night. Although access to information can be very helpful, it can also be enormously distressing and, at times, may even feel disempowering. When we take our ordinary parenting wonderings to the search bar, we may unwittingly end up in an information black hole which provides us with far more than we were looking for. Oftentimes, our attempts to understand something better ends up compounding rather than alleviating our worries. That's where Krysten's Instagram account and this book come in. She has done the work of collecting, preparing, and sharing insight so that we can put it into everyday action. As you'll see, her ability to take theory and research and break it up into bite-size digestible pieces is exceptional.

The common thread in every chapter of this book is connection. Above all else, Krysten and I value relationship because we understand that it is the container for healthy emotional growth, which ultimately leads to living happier, more fulfilled lives. When we're consistently reminded to prioritize and take care of the parent-child relationship, we're more likely to set up the conducive conditions required for true learning and spontaneous growing. Not only for children but for ourselves, too. Understanding the basics of human behaviour gives us the ability to shift the way we see behaviour, and so, with new awareness and consistent willingness, we're able to transform our reactions into responses more of the time.

As caring adults, I believe our actions are firmly rooted in our good intentions. Sometimes, though, we are led astray from what our heart knows to be true because we live in a world that tries to hurry development by shaping behaviour and normalizing potentially harmful parenting practices. When we blindly take hand-me-down techniques and justify their use with, "Well, I turned out fine" or, "Everybody does it" as a yardstick, we may inadvertently resort to using 'discipline' techniques that work against the relationship we yearn to have with our children. It's up to each of us to find our courage and walk our own paths as parents. This book offers us support to do this, especially when we realize that what may be considered 'normal' by the majority no longer aligns with what we intuitively recognize as being natural.

Krysten draws on her formal training as a psychologist, her more than two decades of experience working with children and families, and the round the clock practice of nurturing her own three children. Her words are particularly helpful to those who feel intuitively moved to take a more conscious, gentle approach to raising children without ignoring the science of development. She has gone to great lengths to provide us with evidence-based resources to help support our parenting decisions.

Best of all, Krysten has outlined a plethora of common parenting struggles and has generously offered suggestions for how to navigate certain situations. That said, she does not ask or expect us to follow her instructions to a T. Instead, she invites us to use the insight offered and implement it in ways that feel authentic to us because we're the ones who know our children best and love them most. This formidable combination of both her head and heart has positioned her to be more than a trusted parenting expert; she's a wise and caring companion who's committed to being by our side as we navigate our own unique parenting journey.

Thank you, Krysten, for sharing your wisdom, experience, and caring heart with us in this book. I have no doubt that readers, and the children in their lives, will be better for it.

With love,

Bridgett Miller

Author of What Young Children NEED You to Know: How to See Them So You Know What to Do for Them.

Founder of @parentingwithintention on Instagram

INDEX

Guidance from The Therapist Parent

INDEX

3. True Discipline

INDEX

INDEX

Guidance from The Therapist Parent

INDEX

1.

The Foundation

Understanding Brain Development

Children's behaviour can often be frustrating. The tantrums, wanting irrational things, and generally being overly emotional can infuriate parents. The problem is that these behaviours fit perfectly with children's development. Understanding the basics of child brain development and having some insight into why our children behave this way can make a huge difference in how we respond to them. We no longer feel our children are 'naughty' or deliberately trying to drive us crazy. We understand that they are simply doing their best with what they have. Also, if we help them calm themselves and work through what has upset them, we support their positive brain development.

When humans are born, their brains are underdeveloped. If we waited until our brains were developed to be born (like other mammals), we would give birth to a baby with a head the size of a toddler. And nobody wants to do that! Therefore, a lot of human development must happen after birth. Most growth occurs before the age of five, with the first 1000 days regarded as the most significant.

Human brains develop from the bottom up. Starting with the primitive part of the brain that really just keeps you alive, through to the Cortical part of the brain, which is the logical problem-solving centre. But it takes years for this development to happen. This is why we can't expect kids to think logically; that part of their brain literally doesn't function yet. It's a bit like expecting a child to ride a bike before they have learned to walk. They have yet to reach that stage of development.

Perry's Neurosequential Model

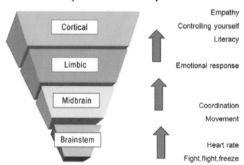

Perry, B.D. (2002) *Brain Structure and Function I: Basics of Organisation. Adapted in part from "Maltreated Children Experience: Brain Development and the Next Generation (W.W. Norton & Company)*

1

I know graphics like the one above can be a little overwhelming. But it is a good visual to understand the progression of brain development. Let's step through that growth now.

Brain stem: 0–6 months: The first part of the brain develops from birth until about six months of age. This part of the brain controls heart rate, breathing, and our 'fight, flight, freez, and fawn' response. This part of the brain requires no 'thinking.' It is simply reactive. When we understand this development, we can more easily see how trauma, even in very young children, can over-develop their 'fight, flight, freeze, fawn' response.

Midbrain: 6 months–2 years: The midbrain is responsible for movement and coordination. It makes sense then that this is the stage when children learn to roll, crawl, and walk. This is when your baby is discovering what their body can do.

Limbic: 2–7 years: This is the part of the brain with which we seem to have the most difficulty. And it is why we have terms like 'terrible twos' and 't(hr)eenagers.' This is the stage of emotional brain development. Where our kids begin to experience big emotions but lack the language and neural connections (brain hardware) to communicate and cope with them. Even when they acquire more language, children spend most of their time operating from the brain's limbic region.

Cortical: 7–adult: Although there is some development from about four years of age, the thinking section of the brain does not become the centre of development until seven years of age. So, if we take a moment to think about this, we can see that our expectations of our five- and six-year-olds may be unrealistic. The prefrontal cortex is the part of our brain that helps us regulate emotions, control social behaviour, problem-solve, and reason. It is helpful to know that this part of the brain is still maturing well into our 20s. Therefore, a child cannot reason the same way an adult does.

What Does This Mean?

This information suggests that unless we recognise our child's stage of development before we try to reason with them, we may be wasting our time. Using logic when they are operating from their limbic brain is not going to help. We need to be patient and compassionate with them.

2

Regardless of how smart you think your three-year-old is, they are not capable of rationally talking about why the blue cup is just the same as the pink cup. They can't think about the fact that the cups are the same and serve the same purpose. All they know is that they wanted the pink cup, but you gave them the blue one. From their limbic operating system, it feels like their world just fell apart. Being in the emotional brain also makes them more reactive to new events. This is why children are comforted by continuity, such as the same-coloured cup. When things change, they can't necessarily predict what will happen, so it can feel like something is wrong.

Before the thinking brain develops, a child can't tell you they feel worried or disappointed about something. Their behaviour is their communication, which they use to let us know something is wrong. Our job is to help them become calm so we can step in as their thinking brain and give them the language for their feelings. They literally can't do this alone. They need us to use our well-developed thinking brains to guide them.

Along with lots of hugs and reassurance, when they are calm, you can name their feelings for them. For example, saying, "You were really disappointed you didn't get the pink cup." When they feel understood, you can bring in some logical thinking. "The pink cup was dirty. That's why I gave you the blue cup." While this may sound unrealistic and time-consuming, fighting with our kids and trying to reason when they literally can't can take even longer. And it usually doesn't work. That's why we must ensure we stay in control and don't fall into operating from our own limbic brains.

Remember, it isn't just toddlers that function from their limbic brain. Whenever we are stressed or anxious, our thinking brain is switched off, and we respond out of instinct and emotion. We have all had moments when we have 'lost it.' In that moment, if someone came up to you and said, "Now that's not logical. Stop crying and get on with it!" Would it help? I'm guessing it would only add fuel to the fire.

Kids are the same. The only difference is that their tolerance for stress and anxiety is far lower than ours, so they are MORE likely to be in their emotional, limbic brain. You can't meet the emotional brain with logic.

3

It simply won't work. You must meet children in their emotions. Let them see that you understand their feelings and help them settle. Only when they are calm will they be able to talk through the problem more logically.

As parents, we don't need to be experts in neuropsychology, but understanding the basics of brain development can free children from our expectations. It also allows us to see our children's behaviour as normal and acknowledge that they need our help to develop these skills, not punish them for developmentally appropriate responses.

We can't expect children to think like adults. They simply don't have this ability. Their emotions are too intense to manage and physically regulate alone. They need us to guide them through emotional situations to a calm state so they can effectively develop these skills.

Instead of expecting a child to meet adult's standard of behaviour, adults need to meet children at their developmental needs

@The_Therapist_Parent

The pencil icon indicates an activity - use a journal or note taking app to work through the activities and record your answers.

Expectations - Deep Dive Questions

So often, we expect too much of our children. For younger kids, this might be expecting they can sit quietly at a restaurant, or share, or adapt to new situations. For older kids, we might expect that they can prioritise and be organised. Or we expect that they can plan ahead, control their emotions, manage anxiety, or be patient with their siblings. See if you can list examples of times your expectations might be too high—especially considering that the logical brain isn't fully developed—then write a sentence or two explaining each one.

Now, think about specific steps you could take to help your child that align more with what they are capable of. For example, instead of expecting your three-year-old to sit quietly at a restaurant, you could have colouring-in or small toys ready (when they are older, I always have a pack of cards in my bag for us all to play before the meal comes). Or you might want to work with your teenager and have regular check-ins to work with them on how to plan and prioritise. List two or three strategies you can use.

Changing the way we do things might need some adjustments to work. How can you support yourself in your new set of expectations? Who else might you need to involve? Will you need to plan for more time in the morning before school to reduce stress? List a few action steps you can take.

5

When we realise that a child's behaviour is due to immature brain development and a natural fight/ flight/freeze response, it's easier to not take it personally. (most of the time)

@The_Therapist_Parent

Sensory Processing as a Key to Behaviour

Many children (and adults) have difficulty processing sensory information. In collaboration with occupational therapists, I have helped kids manage behaviour at school and at home. To recognise sensory processing issues and how they affect behaviour, it is important to have a basic understanding of what they involve. Once we can identify processing issues and appreciate what they reflect, we have a better chance of creating positive behavioural change.

Understanding arousal level and its relation to sensory processing is a relatively new concept, so it is unsurprising that most parents don't yet comprehend its significance. However, when we see that our children's behaviour may be related to their ability to process sensory information, it is like being given a key to unlock their difficulties.

Arousal refers to how alert we are. It is the level of stimulation needed to sustain our attention and perform at our best. We are all different when it comes to our optimal arousal levels. Some people can't cope with any noise while they are trying to think, while others need to have music on constantly.

Meeting our arousal needs depends on how we process sensory information. The critical thing to remember is that some people will need more sensory input than others to be at their optimum state. When our specific arousal needs are met, we can 'self-regulate,' even when our environment changes (we adjust the stimulus or ourselves to receive the stimulation we feel most comfortable with). Self-regulating sensory information can be very difficult for a child. When we work out what their sensory needs are, we can support our children in meeting them.

We process both internal and external information through our senses. Most people understand that we have five senses (sight, smell, sound, taste, and feel), but there are actually eight. We don't often think of balance (vestibular), body awareness (proprioception), and internal awareness (interoception) as senses. However, they contribute significantly to our experience of the world.

7

Understanding each of these senses is crucial for helping a child who is overwhelmed or needs more of one sensation to maintain a balanced level of arousal.

Let's look at them individually.

Visual: While this sense has to do with what we see, it is much more than that. Visual inputs can include the number of objects, the brightness of colours, or the strength and flicker rate of lighting (such as fluorescent bulbs). Some people thrive on having lots of visual stimuli, and find it inspiring. While others can't cope with clutter as they become distracted or even anxious.

Children who get bored at their desks, seem to lack motivation, or not have the ability stay on task, may need more visual input. You could give them a visual timetable of their day and colour code it. A visual timer could also be a beneficial reminder of how long they have to do a task. Even adding colour to their desk could help by providing more stimulation.

However, if your child seems constantly distracted and unable to focus, they may need less visual input. In this case, you need to de-clutter their workspace and move them away from windows. Less colour and natural lighting can provide a more calming environment for people with a lower visual arousal level.

Smell (Olfactory Input): Have you ever smelt something and been instantly transported back to a memory? Scents have a significant impact on us. Some, we find calming, while others can turn our stomachs. Those that have lived in a rural area might love the smell of a truck full of sheep, as it holds fond memories of being on a farm. For most of us, though, it isn't a pleasant smell at all. Odours are everywhere, and we are constantly processing them. If you can't filter them out, the world becomes very overwhelming. Some people seem quite sensitive to aromas, smelling things long before anyone else. Others wear a lot of perfume or are always defusing essential oils. Again, it comes back to the level of sensory input you need for optimum arousal.

Some kids will seek out smells. They may smell objects, clothes, or even people. Unfortunately for them, this is not always socially acceptable. These children tend not to notice strong smells, even when they are very unpleasant. Such kids may benefit from scented pens, play dough, or having essential oils on a tissue in their pocket.

Children who are overly-responsive to smells might find the general mix of smells in a classroom difficult. They may not want to eat near others because of the smell of their food. This can be a challenge because it is hard to eliminate many types of scent. However, for a child like this, you could find a smell they do like and put it on a tissue so they can sniff it when they need to.

Taste (Gustatory Input): We all have a preference for sweet, salty, sour, or bitter foods. But don't leave out the texture and temperature of food or drinks. Have you noticed that you feel more alert when your food is crunchy, or does that make you tired and agitated?

Some kids are very picky eaters. They won't eat certain textures or strong tastes. I have seen children almost vomit because they disliked the texture of mashed potatoes. It might be that your child has trouble controlling the saliva in their mouth, or hates brushing their teeth. Each gustatory input comes with its own arousal level, and it is important to recognise the effect this has. You can encourage children to try new foods, but don't force them. Depending on the level of stimulation they require, kids might crave strong flavours, love crunchy foods, chewing on things, or drinking through a straw. These kids benefit from chewing gum or chewable accessories or toys.

Hearing (Auditory Input): Some people love quiet, while others feel best with music or the radio constantly on. Each person's auditory needs can be very different. Some children find filtering out sounds difficult. They can't distinguish between hearing the teacher and hearing background noises, like the air-conditioner.

Kids can be quite sensitive to particular sounds, such as vacuum cleaners or traffic noise. These kids might be excited to go to a concert, then cry the whole time or cover their ears.

9

This is difficult at school because keeping so many children quiet is hard. If a child finds noise really challenging, they could try noise-cancelling headphones. Also, warning these children that there may be noises, like the vacuum, can help them manage their anxiety.

Other kids will turn the TV up so loud the whole neighbourhood can hear it. Or, if it is quiet, they will make their own noises by tapping, humming, or singing. They are likely to try anything to break the silence. Background music can be helpful for these kids. Chances are, they will also enjoy learning a musical instrument.

Feel (Tactile Input): This sense relates to how we feel about all kinds of touch, including light touch, deep pressure, vibration, texture, temperature, and even pain. Kids who are oversensitive to tactile input might loathe having their hair brushed, feeling the seams in socks, or tags on clothes. They might also dislike playing in sand or getting dirty. At school, these kids will likely need a quiet corner they can go to when they feel overwhelmed. Deep pressure, such as squeezing down their arms and legs, hugs, or pressured vests before they get dressed can help them tolerate their clothes.

Kids who seek touch may doodle or click a pen while listening. They may be constantly touching things or playing rough, and they don't seem to notice when they are touched lightly or if they have food on their faces. These kids don't seem to perceive temperature, wearing shorts and t-shirts in winter when everyone else is rugged up. The best types of stimulation for these children provide a range of tactile elements and textures. You could encourage them to play with sand, dough, or fidget toys. Be careful to ensure that fidget toys meet their sensory needs rather than just distracting them.

Balance/Motion (Vestibular Input): If a child has difficulty with vestibular input, they won't want to go on swings or rides that move fast. They may even avoid elevators and escalators. These children need options for play that are less active, such as board games.

On the other hand, some kids are always upside-down on the monkey bars, doing rolls across the lounge or spinning without getting dizzy.

Building opportunities for movement into the day is especially important for these kids. At school, they could take messages between classes or do physical exercises between activities. Wobble chairs or elastic bands stretched between chair legs that they can kick or bounce on can also be helpful.

Body Awareness (Proprioception): Although this concept is complex, proprioception essentially relates to knowing where you are in space. When you close your eyes, stretch out your hands, and try to touch your two index fingers together, you are using your proprioceptive system. The receptors used for this are in your muscles and joints. Kids that need less proprioceptive input can be seen as lazy or lethargic. They may have poor pencil grip and seem clumsy. Deep-pressure massage may be helpful for these children. Finding a movement exercise that the child considers calming is the most important aspect for children with this arousal level.

Kids who seek an increased proprioception input are often considered hyperactive. They constantly move, are rough, and love jumping and swinging. They may chew their clothes or like to be under many blankets in bed. These kids often feel calmer after heavy-impact work that involves pushing, pulling, or lifting. Most movement activities, including stretching, will benefit kids needing this arousal level. Weighted blankets and compression vests can also be calming for them.

Internal Awareness (Interoception): Interoception is the ability to recognise signals in the body, such as hunger, thirst, itching, the need to go to the toilet, and even emotions. It is worth considering how you usually behave if you are hungry or need to go to the toilet. Chances are, you might be emotionally volatile (hangry, anyone?)

But some kids don't recognise their needs before it is too late. These children may miss the subtle changes in their bodies due to rising emotions until they are at the point of exploding. Kids that need high levels of interoception input may also have a significant tolerance for pain. They may not know when they are hungry or full, and may accidentally wet themselves because they didn't sense that their bladder was full. To help these kids function well, you may need to schedule food, drink, and bathroom breaks for them. You can also explicitly teach them about changes that can be felt in their bodies.

When teaching them how to recognise their body signals, have them draw a picture of their body. If you wanted to focus on the physical changes for emotions, you could go through each one and draw what their body may feel like. You could then number the changes as the emotions get more intense. However, you can help them recognise other physical changes such as needing to go to the toilet. Start with a tiny discomfort right through to 'busting.'

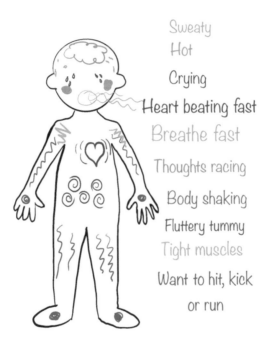

Sweaty
Hot
Crying
Heart beating fast
Breathe fast
Thoughts racing
Body shaking
Fluttery tummy
Tight muscles
Want to hit, kick
or run

Within each of the eight senses, we can be either sensory seeking or sensory avoiding to feel at our optimum state of arousal. If we can consider our child's behaviour in these terms, we begin to realise that they are just trying to get the level of stimulus right. Once they feel comfortable with their arousal, they will feel more balanced. The kid who makes annoying noises probably isn't doing it just to get on your nerves. They may be trying to give themselves the level of auditory input they need. As long as we maintain awareness of this, we can encourage them to meet their needs in a way that doesn't drive everyone crazy!

Comprehending sensory needs and determining stimulus levels will help us appreciate our kids' needs. This understanding means we are more likely to support them to meet these needs appropriately rather than simply overreacting to their behaviour.

It is easy to miss the early signs of dysregulation in a child

if we stay curious about what is behind the behaviour, sometimes we can meet their need before a meltdown

@The_Therapist_Parent

Sensory Difficulties Checklist

Sensory Processing Difficulties

- Tactile defensiveness.
- Tactile seeking.
- Proprioceptive seeking.
- Proprioceptive difficulties.
- Auditory defensiveness.
- Auditory hyposensitivity.
- Olfactory hypersensitivity.
- Olfactory hyposensitivity.
- Visual hypersensitivity.
- Visual hyposensitivity.
- Vestibular hypersensitivity.
- Vestibular hyposensitivity.

1. Tactile Defensiveness/Seeking

Tactile Defensiveness is when someone is overly responsive to tactile input (touch, pressure, temperature or pain).

What it looks like:

- A child becomes dysregulated, upset, or anxious with light and unexpected touch.
- Irritated by certain textures, seams, or tags on clothing.
- Difficulties walking barefoot on certain textures, like sand, grass, or carpet.
- Upset by 'messy play' and may seem to always want to keep hands clean.
- Struggles with textures of soap, lotion, shampoo, etc.

Tactile Sensory Seeking is when someone is under-responsive to touch.
What it looks like:

- They need to touch and feel everything around them.
- Touches people or objects to the point of annoying others.

- They can lack of awareness when their face is messy from food.
- Low reaction to what should be painful.
- Seek out messy or wet tactile play.

2. Proprioception Seeking/ Difficulties

Proprioception: Knowing your body position and limits for weight bearing, stretching, pulling/pushing/lifting against resistance, and movement.

Children engage in proprioceptive-seeking behaviours in order to gain more information about their body position.

What it looks like:
- Constant movement fidgeting, rocking, not being able to sit still.
- Becomes overly excited when needed to use movement.
- Takes risks, e.g. climbing where it is unsafe.
- Rough play or falling on purpose for play.
- Crashes into pillows, or rolls on the floor.
- Wears clothes as tight as possible.
- Might hit, push, or bite others.

Proprioceptive difficulties occur when a child had difficulties with body awareness and what they need their bodies to do.

What it looks like:
- Not knowing how to produce the appropriate amount of force for Lego or connective toys.
- Not knowing the force for writing, colouring, and drawing activities (pushes too hard or too softly).
- Breaks things often.
- Has difficulty handling delicate items.
- Has trouble working out mass, e.g., what is light vs. items that are heavy.

3. Auditory Defensiveness/Hyposensitivity

Auditory defensiveness is when a child is hypersensitive to sound.

What is looks like:

- Upset by unexpected or loud noises.
- May hold hands over their ears often.
- Difficulty concentrating with background noise.
- Finding certain frequencies e.g. a person's voice, car sirens, certain musical pitches, difficult.
- Wants to avoid loud activities such as a movie theatre, large crowds, fireworks, etc.

Auditory hyposensitivity is when a child seeks sound or doesn't register sound.

What this looks like:

- Doesn't respond to their name being called.
- Constantly making sounds themselves.
- Verbal directions need to be repeated.
- Doesn't seem to know where a sound is coming from.
- The volume for music, TV, or devices are always loud.

4. Olfactory Hypersensitivity/Hyposensitivity

Olfactory hypersensitivity is when a child is overly responsive to smells.

What it looks like:

- Refuses to eat foods because of their smell.
- Smells things that others can't.
- Upset by smells that don't bother others.
- May avoid certain places, such as the dentist, because of the smell.

Olfactory hyposensitivity is when a child is under-responsive to smell.

What this looks like:

- Loves foods that have very strong smells.
- Doesn't notice unpleasant odours.
- Smells things or people in an unusual way.
- Difficulty discriminating between different smells.

5. Visual Hypersensitivity/Hyposensitivity

Hypersensitivity to visual input is when a child is over-responsive to visual input.

What this looks like:

- Avoids to bright lights.
- Avoids eye contact.
- Distracted by subtle visual input, e.g. people moving, bright colours.

Hyposensitivity to visual input is when a child is under-responsive to visual input.

What this looks like:

- Trouble with differences in puzzles, pictures, words, or objects.
- Can't seem to find an item amongst other items, such as a food pantry, a full desk, clothes in a drawer, etc.
- Difficulty tracking something moving, such as a ball or a car passing by.
- Doesn't notice all the food on their plate.
- May have difficulties with depth perception.
- Trouble focusing on items with little or no contrast.

6. Vestibular Hypersensitivity/Hyposensitivity

Vestibular hypersensitivity is when a child is overly responsive to vestibular input (position in space, gravitational changes, and sense of movement).

What this looks like:

- Avoids swings, ladders, toy cars, slides, etc.
- Has a fear of heights, even stairs.
- Hates being turned upside down or moving backwards.
- Loses balance easily and can seem clumsy.
- Poor balance and postural control.
- Avoids spinning.
- Fearful of anything where their feet leave the ground.

Vestibular hyposensitivity is when a child is under responsiveness to vestibular input.

What looks like:

- Can spin and not get dizzy.
- Loves swinging for a prolonged period of time.
- Enjoys rollercoasters or other thrill-seeking activities.
- Rocks back and forth when sitting.
- Enjoys being tossed in the air, or upside-down.
- Loves riding bikes, scooters or a skateboards.
- Rocking or nodding their head back and forth.

Remember

This sensory processing difficulties checklist **is not a diagnostic tool**. The aim is to help you better understand the different sensory processing systems, and difficulties to help you understand your child's behaviour. If these behaviours affect their function, development, and their ability to engage in meaningful activity, then it would be best to see an Occupational Therapist who can do a formal assessment of their sensory needs.

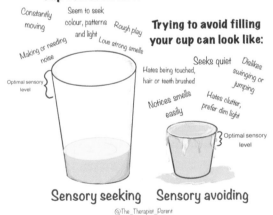

Trying to fill your cup can look like:

Constantly moving

Seem to seek colour, patterns and light

Rough play

Making or needing noise

Love strong smells

Optimal sensory level

Trying to avoid filling your cup can look like:

Seeks quiet

Dislikes swinging or jumping

Hates being touched, hair or teeth brushed

Hates clutter, prefer dim light

Notices smells easily

Optimal sensory level

Sensory seeking   Sensory avoiding

@The_Therapist_Parent

Why Sleep is Vital for Development

We all cherish those moments of peace when our kids are finally asleep, allowing us to recharge, have adult conversations, or enjoy TV that isn't child-friendly. However, fostering a consistent sleep routine and ensuring children get enough sleep offers benefits far beyond our relief for our sanity (although that is a good reason, too).

Sleep is vital for our health, mood, and development, comparable in importance to eating well and exercising. Sleep is directly linked to immune function, growth, concentration, memory, mood, learning ability, and even coordination (Buysse et al, 2010). However, parents commonly face challenges with their children's sleep, such as getting kids to sleep, having them wake several times a night, or early waking. Some parents just give up trying to enforce a routine and adapt their own habits to fit their child's poor sleep style. While this is entirely understandable, especially as a technique to 'survive' and get some much-needed sleep, it is vital to recognise the importance of sleep and why it is such a priority.

Sleep Keeps Us Healthy

Research strongly links sleep to our immune function. During sleep, our body produces infection-fighting proteins called cytokines. Studies indicate that adults getting less than seven hours of sleep per night are three times more likely to catch a cold than those with eight hours of sleep (Mahoney, 2014). Even just one hour less sleep can significantly impact our ability to stay healthy.

Sleep promotes the production of growth hormones, which is why babies sleep for long periods. Their body is doing everything it needs to grow and develop and does so by sleeping.

Concentration and Attention

As adults, we know it is difficult to think clearly when we haven't had enough sleep. A lack of sleep tends to make us more impulsive and unable to fully think through consequences. Consider what this is like for children; logical thinking and impulse control are already limited due to their underdeveloped brains. It would be challenging for a sleep-deprived child to sit in a classroom, listen to a teacher, or complete academic tasks.

Interestingly, the symptoms of Attention Deficit/Hyperactivity Disorder (ADHD) closely resemble sleep deprivation (Owens et al, 2016). With such closely aligned signals, identifying sleep disorders is crucial when evaluating ADHD. A high percentage of children with ADHD also have difficulty sleeping.

Memory and Learning

Studies show that young children perform better and retain more information if they have taken a nap, as opposed to times when they are not well rested (Mahoney, 2014) because it greatly benefits brain function. During sleep, neurotransmitters (chemicals that allow brain cells to communicate) help you remember what you have heard, learned, or seen while awake. Sleep also supports neuroplasticity, enabling the brain to develop new pathways and functions (Dawkins, 2018). So, sufficient sleep allows children's brains to remember what they have learned and form the cognitive pathways that make learning and remembering easier.

Mood

Lack of sleep can make us cranky, with low tolerance levels. In children, especially those with underdeveloped emotion regulation, this results in emotional outbursts that seem to be triggered by the most minor things, which pretty much sums up the overtired child on the floor crying because someone else opened the front door first. However, sleep deprivation can be far more detrimental than this when it comes to mood. Poor sleep is associated with increased levels of anxiety and depression in both children and adults.

Children with sleep disorders often experience excessive brain arousal during sleep, triggering an unnecessary fight-or-flight response. The ripple effect this causes disrupts their hormones, particularly their cortisol (stress hormone) levels, and impacts their mood. A clear example of this was a highly anxious young boy I treated. Having given him strategies to manage his anxiety, which had little effect, he returned one day as a completely different child. He was calm and happy, traits I had never seen him exhibit. In the interim, his parents discovered he had sleep apnea, which had now been treated. This emphasises the profound impact of sleep, as the only thing that had changed was that the boy was getting enough sleep.

20

How Much Is Enough Sleep?

National Sleep Foundation guidelines recommend nightly sleep durations of 12-14 hours for ages one–three, 11-13 hours for ages three–five, and 10-11 hours for ages five–twelve. Individual needs may vary, but research generally supports these timeframes. It is important to note that it doesn't take long for the negative impacts of sleep to become evident in children. Even a one-hour nightly sleep deficit over four nights is enough to negatively impact children's health (Mahoney, 2014). This is a concern to bear in mind, especially during school holidays.

Improving Sleep

There are no magic cures for sleep issues. Improving sleep involves the consistent use of multiple small strategies.

Routine: Sleep needs to happen at the same time every night, so establish a consistent bedtime routine. Our body gets into a rhythm when it comes to sleep, so try to do activities like bathing, brushing teeth, and reading stories at the same time and in the same order each night. This calm time before bed helps the body wind down. While this isn't always going to work, creating these habits enables a child's body to automatically calm through the routine.

Limit Screen Time: Blue light from screens inhibits the body's production of melatonin (which helps regulate sleep) and overstimulates the brain. So, even when we think our kids are calm, sitting quietly watching an iPad, their brains become overstimulated, making it very difficult to sleep. Avoid screens for at least an hour before bed, and definitely keep screens out of the bedroom.

Create an Environment That Promotes Calm: Anxious children often have difficulty calming their thinking enough for sleep. Their thoughts seem to come flooding in when there are no other distractions. These are the kids that come of out their room repeatedly, usually to share something they have remembered or feel is necessary. Telling them they must stay in their room only increases their anxiety. Setting a specific number of times they are allowed to come out can help. Knowing they have this opportunity reduces their anxiety as it enables them to feel heard, and, over time, they may not need to use it as often.

If they always seem to have a lot on their mind, consider having them keep a notebook beside their bed to write down their thoughts. That way, they won't have to keep thinking those thoughts; they are safe in the notebook. Doing controlled breathing or meditation at bedtime will also help their body and brain calm enough to sleep.

While these guidelines are beneficial to prepare the body for sleep, they may not always work. However, if your child experiences consistent sleep problems, help from a paediatrician or sleep specialist is recommended.

Sleep is as crucial to health as nutrition and exercise, and neglecting it or taking it for granted can severely hinder the growth, development, learning, and happiness our children experience.

Telling a child that a nightmare isn't real simply doesn't fit their experience. Their heart was racing, they felt it, to them it was real

@The_Therapist_Parent

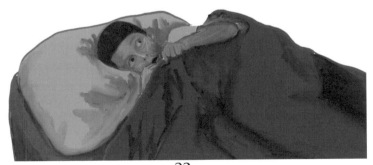

Sleep Tips and Tricks

1. Limit Screen Time: There is much research to show that the blue light emitted from screened devices decreases the body's production of melatonin (Green et al, 2017). Basically, the hormone melatonin helps you go to sleep. When there is blue light, the body thinks it is day time and it stops releasing melatonin so that you will stay awake. I know that parents get desperate and give their kids an iPad in bed to 'calm' them down, but sadly, this actually makes it more difficult for them to sleep. Screens should be turned off at least an hour before bedtime.

2. Calm Together Time: If you spend connected time with your kids before bed, they will likely feel less need to get out of bed and will be more able to sleep peacefully. Try to avoid the bedtime rush. I know that parents may be desperate to get their kids into bed so that they can finally have some time alone. But if we invest a little more time in keeping things calm as the kids go to bed, it is more likely that everyone will get a better night's sleep.

Spend time having snuggles and talking about the day. It is a good idea to add gratefulness to your bedtime routine. Everyone, including parents, can take turns saying what they are grateful for. This focuses everyone's attention on the positives, which is particularly important before sleep. Also, don't skip story time. Reading a story together, even for older children, will help them positively activate their imagination and help them dream.

3. Journal: For older children, journalling can work well to put their thoughts to rest at bedtime. We know that when the distractions of the world have stopped, it can be hard to get your brain to stop, too. Writing down your thoughts gives your brain a break. You no longer feel that you have to remember everything because it is written down. Younger children can journal by drawing what happened during the day.

4. Bedtime Passes: For the kids who constantly come out of bed after you have tucked them in, having a set number of times they are allowed to come out can be helpful. Not only do they feel reassured that they can come out if they need to, but if there is a limit, they can evaluate if they really need to come out. Don't make it too hard. Give them the number of times you are both comfortable with. Make their nightly quota of passes as physical 'tickets' and have them hand one to you each time. Over time, as they get better at this, and you can reduce the number of passes they can use each night.

5. Mailbox: Some kids just find that night is when they remember everything they 'have' to tell you. It feels really important, and they just can't sleep until they tell you. Older kids may be able to journal, but this is too much for younger kids. Have them make a mailbox. Just cover an empty tissue box and cut a flap in the back so you can open and close the box to get the letters out. Have pen and paper next to their bed and if they remember something that they want to tell you, they can write it or draw it and 'mail' it to you. In the morning, you can go through the letters together.

6. Worry Monster: Letting go of worries can be difficult, especially at night, alone in bed. A way that kids can learn to release worries is to make a worry monster. Again, using an empty tissue box, cover and decorate it with the opening as the 'monster's' mouth. The child can then write or draw their worries and 'feed' them to the monster. This activity helps children tangibly notice their thoughts and choose to release them. Obviously, this is a friendly pet monster, but if you don't want it to be a monster it could be a pet dog or other animal your child imagines.

These are just a few strategies that I've used with kids over the years. You need to find what will work for your child. You might like to use a combination, for example, the passes and the mailbox (for when they have run out of passes.) Get your kids involved; what do they think will help? Most importantly, we need to do what is best for our kids and our family, and what that looks like for one family, will be different for another. In the end, this too, shall pass. So, hold on, you will get through it.

Looking Behind the Behaviour

There is so much more to behaviour than we see on the surface. As our most developed form of interaction, we use our behaviour to communicate our needs long before we can talk. Even after we learn to speak, our body still communicates what we are feeling before we are conscious of it, let alone able to articulate it. So, it is up to us to look at what a child's behaviour is really trying to tell us, especially if they have difficulty verbally communicating their feelings or needs.

It isn't always easy to interpret a child's behaviour. Sometimes, it can seem as though their reaction comes out of nowhere. However, if we take a step back and look objectively, there will have been a trigger that set off the change. When trying to decode this behaviour, it can be helpful to use a 'checklist' of possibilities to determine the cause.

Five Common Needs behind a Child's Behaviour

1.   Basic Needs

This might seem simple, but how often have we, as adults, been 'hangry,' and once we've had something to eat, can think clearly and act rationally again. If your body hasn't got what it needs, your behaviour won't be at its best. Children can't always recognise what their body tells them. Have you ever asked a cranky child, "Are you tired?" Their response was probably to scream, "No. I'm not!" Most of the time, they only know that they don't feel good.

When we look at what motivates behaviour, it is good to start with the basics. Is the child tired, hungry, thirsty, cold/hot, sick, uncomfortable, or feeling unsafe? Remember, a child might be physically safe, but they could feel uncertainty, which causes their body to go into a protective state of fight/fight/freeze/fawn. They may be perfectly safe at preschool and even know many people there. But being away from people they feel secure with could trigger feelings of being unsafe, resulting in challenging behaviour.

2. Connection

Connection is more than just being in the same family or having a friend. It is something we all crave because it validates who we are and gives us a feeling of belonging.

25

When we have a connection with someone, we are reassured that we are loved and accepted for who we are. These are the people we trust and can communicate and share our lives with. When a child lacks connection, they become unsettled and unsure, a state bound to cause dysregulation. Remember, a child's feeling of disconnection may not be with you. It could be from a sibling, friends, a teacher, or anyone they desire connection with. If they can't meet their connection need with those people, they will push for it with you.

3. Sensory

In the article *Sensory Processing as a Key to Behaviour* on page seven, I outlined the eight senses (sight, smell, taste, touch, hearing, vestibular, proprioception and interoception) we use to understand our world. When a child's body is over- or under-stimulated, they will do whatever they can to return it to their optimum sensory level. If they are under-stimulated, they will move, fidget, climb, make noise, etc. If they are over-stimulated, they will do whatever they can to avoid the stimulation. They may refuse to participate, hide, or eventually have a meltdown.

4. Feeling Seen and Heard

Feeling seen and heard involves more than just knowing children are around. When a child feels seen and heard, they know that the important people in their life understand who they are, accept them, and value their input. This is how a child experiences the feelings of belonging and being of value. Without this, a child's view of themselves will suffer and, in turn, so will their behaviour. Initially, they will fight to be heard. But eventually, if this need isn't met, they won't expect others to appreciate what they have to offer.

5. Skills

All too often, expectations of how children 'should' behave are far too high. In the article *Understanding Brain Development* on page 1, we discussed expectations in relation to brain development, but we often expect too much of children cognitively, socially, and emotionally as well. Impulse control, for example, doesn't start to develop until about the age of five–seven years. Yet we become frustrated with a young child for acting impulsively.

Understanding social etiquette, sharing, turn-taking, and seeing other's perspectives develops throughout childhood. These are not skills they have from the outset.

Parents often get upset with their children for being disorganised, forgetting what they were asked, and not being able follow directions e.g., clean their room. All of these skills require focus, the ability to hold information, think it through, filter distractions, and plan ahead. Being able to do all of this is what we call executive function. Typically, executive function isn't fully developed till 18–20 years of age. It is no wonder children find this so difficult. Getting angry with a child for not having a skill won't make them have that skill. They need to feel safe and supported so they can learn it through practise.

Identifying the need behind a particular behaviour isn't always easy. It can be especially difficult in the heat of the moment when everyone's emotions are escalated. But practising identifying the motivation will ultimately help you to see your child's reaction as a desperate desire to communicate a need rather than just difficult behaviour.

A child's most developed form of communication is behaviour

What their behaviour might be saying.......

I'm overwhelmed

I need you

This doesn't feel right

I'm tired/hungry

@The_Therapist_Parent

Looking Behind the Behaviour - Deep Dive

Questions

What does your child do when they are in their 'emotional' brain?

Here is a list of common responses, circle the ones that most often apply to your child and add your own.

Screaming

Whining

Sulking

Crying

Hurting themselves

Slamming doors

Throwing things

Gritting teeth

Sarcasm

Hitting

Refusal to communicate

Flushed face

Yelling ("I hate you!" or, "You're so mean")

Clenched fists

Stomping feet

Rolling eyes

Inability to talk, (groans, grunts)

Physical complaints (stomach aches, headaches)

Loud

'Silly' behaviour

Climbing all over you

Overactive

What else do you notice in your child?

Which of these behaviours are the first signs that your child is becoming dysregulated?

These behaviours are messages that your child sends to let you know that their brain isn't in a state of integration, and that they need help before they escalate. What need is their behaviour trying to communicate?

Basic Needs: Are they hungry, thirsty, tired, uncomfortable, or feeling unsafe?

- When did they last eat or drink?
- Have they had a lot on or lack sleep?
- Are they getting sick?
- Are they comfortable?
- Did plans change (or anything that could make them worry)?

Connection: Are they needing reassurance, belonging, and safety?

- Am I giving them my full attention?
- Have they had a fight with someone?
- Have we had intentional time together?
- Are they having issues with friends?

Sensory: Are they overwhelmed or under-stimulated?

- Is there noise/smells/busyness?
- Too light/dark?
- Have they been able to move their body?
- Are they physically comfortable?

Seen and Heard: Needing to feel like they are important, included, and understood.

- Have I rushed them through their feelings?
- Have they had to go to activities without having a say?
- Have I made space to talk about what they want to talk about?

Skills: Their capability to be successful, whether developmental, physical, cognitive, or social.

- Have I given them instructions with too many steps?
- Do they need help to complete the task?
- Am I expecting too much?
- Is this developmentally appropriate?

When trying to bring your child back state of regulation, we first have to check in with how we are feeling.

How does your body feel when your child is dysregulated? What are you thinking? How do you feel afterward, when things are calm again?

Now, think of your child's behaviour as one of the needs we listed. What are your thoughts and thinking like now?

We have to retrain and re-wire our brains to see the need behind the behaviour, rather than going with our automatic trigger response which we listed first. This doesn't happen instantly. Just like learning anything, it takes repetition and practise. It can help to learn to recognise our first body response (as you listed first) and use this as a signal to STOP before you react. Your body will still go into a protective state, but we can learn to not let it take over. Having a mantra or reminder can be helpful.

- This is not an emergency.
- They are doing the best they can.
- We are safe.
- They need my help.
- It's not personal, it's developmental.

What others could you use to help?

Remember, you can take a break to calm yourself if you need to before you help your child. Do some breathing, a quick burst of exercise, or some form of release to switch your nervous system from fight/flight/freeze/fawn into being able to think logically again.

Once we are calm, we can then help our child calm and meet the need they are showing in their behaviour. When we practise not being triggered (it will still happen but the intensity will decrease), it is easier to look behind the behaviour. You will also get better at seeing the signs before you child has a meltdown and meet that need before they have to ask with their behaviour.

Developing Impulse Control

One of the most frustrating parts of being a parent is how impulsive your children can be. They do and say things without thinking, even when you have told them not to. They don't stop asking for a toy, or just take it without asking. They say the most embarrassing things in public and touch EVERYTHING. But that is exactly what they are supposed to do. As difficult as it is for us, children are supposed to be impulsive. The irritation experienced stems from the fact that our expectations are higher than the children's abilities.

The human brain isn't fully developed until we are well into our 20s. It is constantly growing, changing, and learning. The part of our brain designed to control our impulses doesn't really come online until children are nearly five years old and even then, it is a bit hit and miss. Then just when you think your children have finally gotten a hold of impulse control, right around puberty the brain goes through another huge change in development. Therefore, with adolescence comes poor impulse control again, with the added bonus of hormones! As hard as it is, they are doing their best with what they have at the time.

When a child is in the moment, especially if emotions are high, and they haven't developed the ability to stop and examine the environment, they can't possibly think of the potential consequences and use this information to decide if it is the right time to act. If you ask them why they did what they did, they can't tell you; they just reacted in the moment. With practice and support, we can help children to develop these skills, but just like learning to read, it takes time.

Developing Impulse Control
Some children will naturally have more ability to manage impulses than others. Then there are children with Attention Deficit/Hyperactivity Disorder or other neurodivergence that makes impulse control incredibly difficult. While there are strategies we can put in place to help develop impulse control, some children will still need quite a lot of scaffolding to achieve this. The following steps can be helpful in achieving this aim.

1. Labelling Feelings:

When they are little, children can become overwhelmed with emotions that seem to crash over them like a wave. They have no control over them and they don't really understand what the feeling is. It is our job as parents to label the emotion for them. Just like learning to speak, children need to learn the language of emotions. They need to connect the feeling of anger with their heart racing, getting hot, or wanting to yell and kick. When we can name a feeling, it can become less scary and more normal, something that we all experience.

There is scientific research that explains why labelling feelings is helpful. When we are in a highly emotional state, our limbic or emotional brain takes over. We can no longer think clearly and logically. Our brain is in survival mode and will do what it needs to; either fight, flight, freeze or fawn, and no amount of someone reasoning with us will do anything to change that. However, research has found that if we can label the emotion, we will start to activate the prefrontal cortex or the thinking part of the brain (Lieberman et al, 2007). So basically, when you or your child are overwhelmed by an emotion, simply being able to say what that emotion is will slow the emotional roller coaster and start the process of helping you think clearly enough to find a solution. You don't have to label the emotion in the moment, but do talk about emotions often, read books about them, use visuals (like the Feelings Faces Discs from my website) and help children understand what they feel like. That way when strong emotions do come, they will be more likely to tell you what they are feeling and be able to slow the impulse.

2. Make Directions Clear:

Children struggling with impulse control are easily distracted by taking in all the information around them. We aren't doing them any favours by giving them instructions with multiple tasks. Saying, "Go and get the hairbrush, put your lunch in your bag, and pick your clothes up off the floor," might be too much for them to take in. Keep it simple. To help them focus and ensure they are processing what you have said, have them repeat the instructions back to you. You could even display regular tasks as visual reminders to keep them on track. This kind of visual cue is helpful as the instruction is permanent. When an instruction is spoken, it is easily lost, as the child has to rely on their limited working memory to hold that information. If it is written, they can go back and check it should they get distracted.

3. Problem-Solve Together:

Learning to problem-solve is an incredibly powerful tool to improve impulse control. When we support our children to try to find solutions for themselves (rather than us swooping in and giving them all the answers), we are helping them develop an understanding of possible consequences and the confidence that they have some control over their life. It can be as simple as working out how to build a tower with blocks, but instead of us saying, "No, that won't work, do this other thing instead," we step back and say, "I wonder what will happen if you do that? What else could you do?" Whenever you can, have your children think about what they could do and allow them the time to come up with as many possibilities as they can. Have them think about what would happen if they chose that possibility, good or bad, so they can see why some choices are better than others. For more information on this you can go to chapter *Teaching Problem-Solving,* on page 272.

4. Mindfulness:

Mindfulness is the act of consciously bringing yourself back to the present moment. It entails being aware of your senses, thoughts, and emotions in that moment and not letting your thoughts wander from them. Mindfulness helps build neurological pathways that promote focus and cognitive control. These skills are accessed from the prefrontal cortex of the brain. As most development of the prefrontal cortex takes place in childhood and adolescence, practising mindfulness at these key stages of development helps children build the paths for increased focus, control, and emotional regulation that will stay with them throughout their lives.

There are lots of mindfulness activities you could do. You can help them learn to slow their breathing and connect to their senses. Have them identify what they can see, hear, feel, smell, and taste. Or, simply blow bubbles slowly and watch the colours as they pop. Making these activities fun and doing them regularly will help children connect with how their body feels. And if they practise when they are calm, they will be more likely to be able to do this when they are dysregulated. For more mindfulness activities you can read the *Mindfulness for Children* chapter starting on page 188.

34

5. Impulse Control Games:

Children's games that require listening, following instructions, and stopping are fantastic for developing impulse control.

Games such as Simon Says, Follow The Leader, or Statues all require children to focus on what is happening and respond accordingly. These fun games actually help to build skills in impulse control. More ideas can be found in the activity section that follows.

There are lots of things we can do throughout our days that can help children develop impulse control. But it is important we remember that our children are still growing and developing. We can't expect them to use skills that they simply don't have. They aren't trying to annoy us or not listen; they just don't have the skills yet. But, as we support them and practise these skills with them, they will eventually develop impulse control.

The part of the brain that helps with impulse control doesn't come online till about 4 years and then offline again at puberty.

They really are doing the best they can

@The_Therapist_Parent

Impulse Control Activities

Impulse control is an important skill to learn, and the earlier children start practising it, the better at it they'll become. While we need to teach them, it doesn't have to be through boring lessons. One of the best ways to learn impulse control is through playful games. Here are a few ideas.

1. Role-Playing Impulse Control

Role-play is a great way to model and practise self-control and impulse control in different situations. It means that you can tailor the scenarios to suit the difficulties your child might have at the time. It's also a great way to promote listening skills and empathy, as they can role-play the parent or other children in the scenario and experience how others feel. You could play out when your child wants something at the supermarket, when they call out in class or whatever situation seems to need practise at the time. Be careful not to shame your child. You want them to have empathy, but not feel responsible. They are learning and this is a way for them to learn, not a punishment.

2. Statues

For this game, you just need some music and dancing. Play the music and let kids dance however they like while the music is playing. Then, stop the music suddenly. As soon as the music stops, kids should stand absolutely still like a statue; anyone who moves while the music is silent is out of the game.

3. Simon Says

The classic game, Simon Says, combines listening and impulse control skills. This can build better body control and self-control over time. One child is 'Simon' and stands in front of the others. This child gives instructions to the others. If they begin their instruction with "Simon says..." the other children have to follow the instruction, e.g. "Simons says, put your hands on your head." If the child gives the instruction without first saying "Simon says," the children are not to follow the instruction. If they follow when "Simon says" wasn't said, that child is out of the game.

4.Red Light, Green Light

Children have to run from one side of a space to another. When a child hears the words, "Green light!" they can move forward. When they hear "Red light!" they freeze. First one to the other side wins, but if they move during a 'red light' they have to move back to the start. You can add a twist to make it trickier. You can reverse the rules. Make "Red light!" the cue to go, and "Green light!" the cue to stop. This tests a child's ability to go against habit. They need to stop their impulses and practise self-regulation.

5. Board Games

Board games are a fun activity for the whole family. Make sure you choose a game that is relevant to your child's age range and interests. If you read the directions, ask your child to summarise them to practise their verbal comprehension. Board games require patience, taking turns, and problem-solving, and are an easy way to practise learning to win or lose.

2.

Connected

Relationships

What is Connection and Why is it Important?

If you have looked at parenting sites or read any parenting books, you have probably heard the term 'connection.' It seems everyone suggests that 'connection is key' and you should 'connect before you correct.' But what does that even mean?

When professionals use words like connection, you wonder if it has a deeper, unknown meaning. The word is thrown around as if it is a universal parenting term that should be well understood. The truth is, connection is really quite simple. It refers to the feelings you have for the special people in your life. You feel connected when you can genuinely be yourself and know these people love you, no matter what. Connection arises from moments you laugh so hard together that it feels like nobody else is around, or when you can be upset and know that you won't be rejected because of it. It is when you feel heard, understood, and valued. No wonder connection is so important.

According to Daniel Siegel (2001), relationships that honour connection support the development of social, emotional, and cognitive functioning. This research has also found that children with a parent-child connection throughout childhood are healthier, have better relationships, and are less likely to be involved in crime or teenage pregnancies.

When we comprehend that being connected involves having someone who understands you and will be with you regardless of what else happens, it is easy to see why this research makes sense. If you feel safe, valued, trusted, and heard, you are more likely to make better choices. Through connected relationships, children grow to make decisions, not out of fear of punishment but with the values they have received from the connected parent. As they feel more confident in themselves, they are more likely to do what they think is right rather than be swayed by peers.

Unfortunately, it is easy to take connections for granted. The bonds you have in your relationships are not permanent.

Disconnection happens when we don't continually work on our relationships or when something hurtful happens to break trust. Keeping connection strong doesn't mean we have to make ostentatious gestures; the strength is built on small moments throughout the day. However, it is easy to be too busy providing the basics throughout the day that we forget the importance of these small moments of connection.

Building Connection

Empathy

Empathy is essential for building connections. How can you help your child feel heard if you aren't willing to see things from their point of view? When we recognise how they are feeling, even if those feelings make no sense to us, we free them to fully experience their emotions. This freedom arises when they know they can express themselves and maintain their connection with us regardless. It may be that your two-year-old is upset because they have the wrong coloured cup, or your 11-year-old's hair 'isn't working.' Letting them experience the emotion, helping them feel understood, and allowing them to move through it safely is a powerful way to connect with your child. You are their safe place.

Touch

Touch is often overlooked, but it is the physical manifestation of our connection. It doesn't have to be long cuddles (although these are good too). It can be as simple as having your hand on your child's arm or tussling their hair. It also creates intimacy, as you need to enter someone's personal space to make this connection.

We know that touch is vital during infancy for a child's cognitive and physical development, and this need doesn't change throughout the lifespan. Studies have shown that a lack of nurturing touch is associated with childhood difficulties such as anxiety, depression, and behavioural problems (Whiddon and Montgomery, 2011.) Obviously, we don't want to cross personal boundaries. If a child doesn't like to be tickled or touched in a certain way, then respect that. Unwelcome touch does not bring connection. In fact, it can be very damaging.

Fun

Engage your child in play, art, singing, dancing, sport, reading, or whatever they find fun. When we spend time with our kids doing activities they enjoy, we send the message that their interests are important. In these circumstances, we must give our children our full attention and be present with them. Follow their lead and join them in their play. Let them direct you and have a sense of control, as this encourages them to trust you, and they feel valued that you trust them. Engage in their world and with their play. When you go to the park, don't just sit on a bench. Go on the swing next to them or chase them. Most importantly, have fun.

Don't stop having fun as your kids get older, either. Just change the way you play. They probably won't want to play dolls, but they may laugh at you trying to do some of their dance moves. Play their video game, listen to their music, and enjoy the time together. The silly moments are magic when it comes to connection.

Through Correction

It may seem strange to say that correction can bring connection, but this is a significant form of connection. Connection doesn't mean giving your child everything they want to keep them happy. Connection is being real with each other and, despite mistakes and raw feelings, still showing, feeling, and being loved. Through correction, your child can see that even if you are angry or disappointed with their behaviour, your love for them will not change. There is no greater security than knowing that, despite our faults, we are loved and accepted. For this reason, connected parenting does not use punitive forms of discipline when a child needs correction. Instead, you explain to each other how you feel and solve the problem together.

Fun Connection Ideas

Connection can come from many little moments throughout the day. It doesn't have to take up large chunks of your time or involve deep conversations. Here a few fun and simple connection activities:
- Tickling (if they enjoy it).
- Back massages.
- Dancing, the sillier, the better.

- Going for a walk.
- Playing eye spy in the car as you drive.
- Cooking together.
- Reading books together.
- Playing sports together.
- Playing board games or card games.
- Get creative, do painting or craft.
- Pull silly faces at each other.
- Pillow fight.
- Bedtime cuddles.
- Let them do your hair.
- Have some one-on-one time.
- Paint each other's fingernails.
- Watch a movie together.
- Go on a special 'date' together.
- Laugh at private 'in-jokes.'

Chances are, you are already doing a lot of these things. But it does help to be intentional and aware of our children's need for us to meet them where they are. This way, they can grow to feel valued, loved, and confident in who they are.

You can have the best wisdom to share with your child but without a connected relationship, they won't hear it. When they feel seen then they can hear

Connection - Deep Dive Questions

When a child is upset, logic won't work until we've connected to their emotional needs and helped them calm. Connecting with a child's feelings can be a hug, empathetic facial expressions, and using a calm/kind tone of voice. This allows your child to 'feel seen and heard' before you begin trying to solve problems or work through the issue.

What Connecting Does Not Look Like

It can be really hard to connect to a child that has triggered us. Sometimes, with the best of intentions, we say the 'right' things in the 'wrong way.' For example, saying, "I can tell you're really mad right now," but expressing it through gritted teeth and with a harsh tone. Connection is more than just kind words or labelling the emotion. Kids need to feel the connection, like we really understand the situation and care about how they feel.

Now, think about times when you have tried to respond to your upset child without connection.

Non-verbal communication is really important for connection. Think about how you usually use non-verbal communication in these situations.

Eye Contact: For connection, get down to the child's level (or lower) and help them feel safe. Or disconnection, stand over them looking down at them; this is a threatening position.

Facial Expression: For connection, have 'soft' eyes and a relaxed face. Sometimes we don't even realise we are frowning.

Tone of Voice: A calm, soft, and comforting voice will help with connection. A tense, loud, or angry voice will bring disconnection, even if we say the 'right' things.

Posture: If we look calm, our children will feel it. If we have arms crossed, hands on hips etc., they won't listen to what we are saying; only feel what our body is 'saying.'

Gestures: A child will often respond to gentle touches or an offer of a hug. They will become defensive if we point our finger or throw our arms up in the air.

Timing of Response: Children deserve respect, even if we think they are being unreasonable. Let them finish what they are saying before we speak. If we are interrupting, they won't feel valued and this will damage connection.

Intensity of Response: Speaking calmly and being patient will give them a sense of safety so they can calm. Having intense responses, such as yelling, crying etc. are scary and the child will stay in a fight/flight/freeze response.

Bodily Movement: Being close, having relaxed movements, and bending down help the child feel close to you. Walking away quickly, stomping, etc. will bring disconnection.

How Would It Feel For Us?

Think about a time when you were upset or going through something really hard. Imagine you told someone close to you about it. When you did, they argued with you, told you that you shouldn't be upset, tried to distract you, said you were just tired, or should stop making such a big deal about it. How would you feel? What would you body feel like (muscles, jaw, stomach, heart)? How would you respond? Would you argue? Would you shut down? Would you trust them next time you're upset? Would you feel safe and supported? Write down what this would be like.

Now, think about how this situation would have gone if they used connection. Would they validate how you feel? What might they do to soothe and comfort you?

How could you use this example to help you connect with your child when they are upset?

Co-regulating with Children of All Ages

If you have searched what co-regulation is, chances are that you have found information about attaching with your baby. The information will often focus on its development and how trauma (or broken attachment) can affect a child's ability to regulate their emotions. This early learning and attachment to a caregiver is very important in helping the child develop and learn to regulate. But co-regulation shouldn't stop; it is a lifelong strategy. At every stage of development and into adulthood, there are times when emotions are completely overwhelming and we need support and calming from another person.

For the purpose of this article, I will focus on co-regulation between a child and an adult. In its simplest form, co-regulation describes the interaction between a child and another person (not necessarily a parent) where the adult 'shares their sense of calm' when the child is overwhelmed (losing it) or 'dysregulated.' We co-regulate by offering a warm, calm response. Such a response provides support, coaching, and modelling of effective responses to the situation. In this safe place, children can then learn to understand and express their feelings in a positive way. While it is simple to say, it is not necessarily easy to do. Especially if a child's reaction triggers you, and the last thing you feel you can share is calm.

1. Know Your Triggers

You can't share your calm if you don't have any calm to give! To be effective at co-regulation, you need to be aware of the things that get under your skin. Is it being spoken to disrespectfully, being ignored, or a child's refusal? Why do these things trigger you so much? We know that these behaviours are normal for children. Still, they can send us from being a reasonably calm parent to a yelling, screaming mess.

It can help to think about these situations when you aren't in the middle of your emotions. During the situation, it can feel like the child is deliberately trying to drive you crazy. We take it personally because we are so invested in these little people. But the truth is, the kids are just responding from their own emotions; they aren't out to upset you.

2. Focus on the Emotions

Once we can hold back from being triggered ourselves, we then need to take a step back and focus on the child's emotion rather than their behaviour. If a child is yelling at you or even swearing, focus on the anger, not how it is delivered. Pointing out what they are doing wrong will only add fuel to the fire. If you meet this anger with your own, you will only escalate the situation. Instead, say something like, "You seem really angry about this." Acknowledging the emotions brings the focus back to the source of the problem, and from there, you will both have a better chance of finding an acceptable resolution.

3. Keep It Calm

I'm not suggesting that it is easy, but we need to keep ourselves calm when a child has dysregulated emotions. Taking some deep breaths and using a calm voice will definitely help. Yelling when your child is yelling simply doesn't work. What it does do is reinforce that this is an acceptable way to manage our emotions. We all lose it sometimes, and you should not feel guilty if this happens to you. Most of us are doing the best we can with the emotional resources we have at the time. But we can all improve the way we react at times, and in doing that, we are modelling how emotional management can be achieved.

If you respond to yelling with a slow, calm voice, eventually, the child will bring their voice down too. Your tone of voice and body language make a big difference. If you are trying to use a calm voice through gritted teeth and clenched fists, you aren't calm, and it probably won't help. If you need to take a break first, then do that so that when you come back, you can be in control of your own emotions.

4. Emotion Coach

Once you have met your child calmly and acknowledged how they feel, sit with those feelings for a moment. Let the child gain an understanding of how they feel in that moment. This is how kids learn what their emotions are. When we coach them through these feelings, they begin to understand that emotions can be calmed, and they can get help to do this. You might need to sit in silence or let them rant about everything they feel caused the emotions. You might receive the pointy end of this if they believe their feelings are your fault. But stay calm. They are not thinking clearly at this point.

Stay with the acknowledgment of the emotion until their response has settled.

Once they have calmed a little and are able to think clearly, invite them to problem-solve with you. Ask them, "What can we do?" or, "What could we do next time?" Make sure you let them do most of the problem-solving. This is not the time to lecture. The child will just switch off. However, if they are calm enough, you can explain how you felt and what you hope could happen next time.

5. Connection Is Always Key

Co-regulating with your child can actually be an opportunity for connection. Through it, they can be real with us in a very raw way, and we still show unconditional love. It is an opportunity for closeness. If we have been working on building connection, when co-regulation is needed, it will flow more smoothly because the trust has already been built.

Look for opportunities to connect with your child, no matter their age. Let them direct the connection. Whatever they love, be it cricket, art, Thomas the Tank Engine, or Dora the Explorer, use that as a catalyst. You can't expect a child to meet you in your world; you must meet them in theirs. Spend time talking to them about their interests; this shows that you care about them even if you don't share that interest. Have fun together; play games, blow bubbles, have movie nights, or toast marshmallows over a fire. Even just reading a book together builds connection. If that connection is there, co-regulation will be much easier when it is necessary.

Learning to co-regulate with your child is a skill you can draw on during stressful times. It allows children and adults to manage emotions while maintaining connection. It also helps children grow up with a sense of security. Eventually, most people learn to self-regulate - something everyone can benefit from, regardless of age.

To be able to co-regulate with a child we need to build connection and trust. We have to meet them in their world not expect them to come into ours

49

Co-regulation Activities

Co-regulation is how effective self-regulation develops. These skills wire the brain for safety, the ability to soothe anxiety, and general whole-brain development.

Remember, the key to co-regulation is the fact that we are regulated to start with. Your child's nervous system will sync with yours. That's why it is so important to be able to calm ourselves. Once you are calm, and you have been curious with your child about how they feel, you can move on to helping them calm with you. Helping them feel safe and connected is always the first priority.

Here are a few ideas:

1. Breathe Together

Breathing exercises don't have to be complicated, it can be as simple as breathing slowly and having your child match your breath. Hold them (if they will let you) and allow them to feel the rhythm of your breath and join you. The following are fun breathing exercises you can try.

- Pretending to smell a flower and then blowing out candles.

- Shape breathing (I have breathing cards that can help with this). For square breathing, you can trace a square with your finger, inhale as you go up one side, hold at the corner, exhale as you go to the next side etc.

- Nostril breathing: Have your child place their finger over one nostril, then breathe in deeply. Switch your finger to the other nostril as you breathe out. Once you have exhaled slowly, switch nostrils and repeat.

- Finger breathing: Have your child trace the fingers of one hand with the pointer finger of their other hand. As they trace up the finger, have them breathing in, hold at the top of the finger and then breathe out as they trace down (I have a mindfulness puzzle that helps with this and adds visualisation.)

2. Calm Their Senses

This activity depends on what your child's sensory needs are. If your child calms with pressure, a weighted blanket, tight hugs, or swaddling them in a blanket can have a containing and soothing effect. If they like soft touch, rubbing their back and snuggles can help.

You can also create a relaxing atmosphere by lowering the lights and noise level in the house or by playing some relaxing music if they respond to this. Sensory toys or playdough can also help ground the senses and nervous system and settle a brain in overwhelm. But remember, what works for one child won't necessarily work for another. You know your child best. The goal is to help them regulate, so do what you need to do. Everything else can be done once they are calm.

3. Connect through Touch

Touch is a powerful way to connect emotionally with your child, but only if they are ready to respond to touch. Make sure you ask and never force touch. If it's ok, rub their back, feet, hands, or draw simple shapes or pictures on their backs, and then ask them to do the same on you.

4. When Your Child Doesn't Want to Be Touched

If your child is completely melting down, and touch would escalate them, then please don't touch them. While co-regulation often involves sitting together, hugging etc., if that isn't going to work for your child then don't force it. Sometimes, the above strategies may have worked when your child was becoming dysregulated, but not once they reached the point of meltdown or have gone beyond that point. If your child is hitting etc., then you can't allow that. You need to make it clear, "I can't let you hit me, I am here if you need me." Stay close by and offer reassurance, "I can see this is really hard for you. I am here when you need me." This is still co-regulation, even without touch. If you can stay calm (which can be really, really hard), they will still respond to your calm. Eventually, they may want to do some of the other techniques. It is important to practise co-regulation when they are calm and talk about what you could both do when they are dysregulated.

3.

True Discipline

Cooperation, Not Obedience as a Goal of Parenting

We all want our children to do what we ask. Life would be simple if they just did what we asked when we asked it, right? But that's not the goal of parenting; well, it shouldn't be. Our goals should focus on helping our children fully develop their abilities, realise their own values, and constructively problem-solve difficulties they encounter. They can't do this by mindlessly doing what we say. We can't expect children just to do what we want. They are human beings with emotions and opinions of their own. Effective parenting works towards cooperation, not obedience.

How Is Cooperation Different To Obedience?

If your expectation is obedience, then chances are you often engage in a power struggle. Yelling, punishments, manipulation, and fear become how you get your child to do what you want. These actions often lead to children pushing boundaries as they try to gain control and independence. The power struggles then escalate. Or, such reactions will cause blind obedience, which can be much worse.

We must stop and think, is blind obedience really what we want? Do we want a child who will grow up to be someone who will just do as they are told? Never challenging authority, peer pressure, or being mistreated? Of course not. Like it or not, we are our child's practise space for life. As a safe place, we are likely to experience more intense conflict at times; but that doesn't have to be a bad thing. Our job is to teach our children HOW to have their say and question decisions when needed.

Cooperation, on the other hand, means that your expectations are explained, and you invite your child to think of ways to meet these. It doesn't mean that your child does whatever they want. It does, however, mean that they are given choices and some control over their actions. There are still boundaries, but you work things out together rather than taking a 'my way or the highway' attitude.

How To Foster Cooperation:

Explain the Rules: Of course, you need to have rules. We want our kids to grow and be adults that share our values. Make your expectations clear when talking to your child and explain why. A child is more likely to follow a rule if they understand why we have that rule in the first place. Would you say "No" to your partner without explaining why? Or say, "Because I said so?" We wouldn't because it is disrespectful and confusing. The same is true for children. We don't have to give long-winded explanations, but some reason is definitely helpful. It could be that they need to unpack the dishwasher. You can explain that in a family, everyone needs to help each other, and one way is sharing the jobs. Emptying the dishwasher might be their job. Or, you could explain that you are saying "No" to a request because you are tired. Giving your child some context can often help them understand or at least accept the situation.

Give Them Some Control: As adults, we can forget that children are people too. Just like us, children don't like to feel manipulated and powerless. When children start to say "No," they are gaining independence and beginning to realise they have choices. Although it might seem defiant at times, this is a positive stage in their development. If we can recognise that our children just want some control, we will see that taking control away from them might result in unwanted outcomes. This doesn't mean we just give in to them so they can experience control. But we can give them choices. For example, if your child says "No" when you tell them to have a shower, offer them the choice of showering before or after dinner. For young children, the choice might be as simple as choosing the plate they eat off, even though they can't choose the foods they get for dinner. They are still doing what you want, but they feel that they have some control.

You can also acknowledge their perspective. When kids feel understood, they're more able to accept our limits. Remember that it is difficult for all of us to follow the rules sometimes. If possible, give your child a choice or a redirection about what they CAN do to meet their needs or solve their problem. For example, if your child wants to keep playing at bedtime, the following conversation could be helpful, "I can see you wish you could play longer. It's hard to stop playing and get ready for bed, isn't it? Would you like to choose a book for us to read in bed?"

54

Is It Worth the Fight?: There are some situations where it really isn't worth the fight. In these situations, let your child live with the natural consequences. If your child refuses to wear a jacket, let them go out and experience the cold. This way, they learn for themselves, and you don't have to enter into a yelling match. Obviously, you can't do this if the consequence is dangerous, but if it is just discomfort, then let them decide.

You need to work out what your core values are and what behaviours you really need them to do, then let go of some of the more trivial things. These are not worth fighting over. Do you want your children to be kind? Do you value helpful children? Are you appreciative when they give you some space when you need it? When you realise what is really important to you, you can let go of other battles, like them wanting to wear a superhero cape or mismatched clothes.

Problem-Solve Together: If you find that you and your child are butting heads regularly over the same issue, then you must work through it together. If you don't engage your child in this process, you are just setting yourself up for another power struggle. Sit down with your child when you are both calm and simply explain that things aren't working. Have them try to come up with ideas about what else could happen. If you don't think the ideas will work, then talk through what would happen if you did carry them out. Offer suggestions but be willing to listen if they have a problem with your proposal. You may have to bend a bit. Remember, having them obey you without question is not a win; they will only feel controlled and want to rebel. Having them come up with ideas that you can both agree on not only means they are more likely to comply, but also, they are more likely to feel valued.

One of the most effective influences we have on our children is our relationship with them. If we are trying to teach (discipline) our children, we are providing opportunities for them to learn and grow, it is not done to harm or criticise. When disciplining a child, sit with them and explain what rules were broken. Describe the consequence and problem-solve with them as to how they can fix the situation. By doing this, we are working together as a team rather than with an 'us vs them' mentality.

We show we understand how they felt, and we also talk about how we, or others in the situation, felt as well. By acknowledging everyone's feelings, we connect with them and build understanding.

Obedience has long been the goal of parenting, but I ask that you challenge this belief. In the long-term, obedience can often bring more harm than good. Our goal as a parent is to help our children grow and develop their own values, beliefs and convictions. If we want them to grow to be independent adults who will make right decisions and not blindly follow, we cannot enforce obedience. We have, instead, to develop cooperation.

Parenting keys

@The_Therapist_Parent

Relationship comes first

Co-regulation to calm emotions

Work through solutions together

Cooperation - Deep Dive Questions

Wouldn't it be wonderful if when we asked our children to do something, they'd instantly jump up with a smile on their face, say "Sure," and do it straight away every single time. But that's not realistic. While nothing will encourage cooperation every time, there are things we can do to lower frustration and increase the chance that children will listen and cooperate.

Start by thinking of a situation that you and your child particularly struggle with. What is it you want them to do? What do they do and how does it usually end?

1. Check Your Expectations

Is what you are asking developmentally appropriate? Are you giving too many instructions at once? Does this task require planning, memory, and thinking ahead? Are they able to do this?

2. How Are You Asking?

The way we ask makes a big difference. A good way to check how you speak to your child is by putting yourself in their shoes. If your partner said, "Go and clean your room NOW!" how would you respond? Children are just like us; they get defensive and defiant when there are demands. You can still be firm and kind. Tone, body language, and how close you are standing to your child all make a difference. Is there anything you could change?

3. Have You Explained Why?

Expecting anyone to do what they are told without question or understanding is a lot to ask. Have you explained why they need to do what you are asking? How could you give them more information?

4. Can They Have Some Control?

Having some control helps children (and adults) take ownership of what needs to happen and means that they are more likely to do what you ask. Can they have some control over when the task needs to be done or how it is done?

If not, what controls can you give them, e.g. can they choose the book to read at bedtime after they clean their teeth? Write down what control they can have.

5. Problem-Solve Together

If you and your child are consistently struggling with same issue, then you need to come together and work through it. Sit down with your child when you are both calm and explain that things aren't working. Ask them to try to come up with ideas about what else could happen. If you don't think their ideas will work, then talk through what would happen if you did do what they suggest. Offer your suggestions, but be willing to listen if they have a problem with what you are saying. You may have to bend a bit, but as long as it still gets done, you can let the little things go. How could you compromise?

Why Punishment Doesn't Work and What Does

Surely, we have to punish our kids? If we don't, they will become spoiled brats, right? Wrong. This is probably one of the biggest misconceptions in parenting. Psychologists over the years haven't helped with this belief. Historically, the focus of behaviour change has been on rewards and punishments. Society is built on this way of thinking. If we speed in our cars and get caught, we get punished with a fine. Of course, rules can be helpful, but does the punishment actually work?

Consider speeding: my guess is that you have driven over the speed limit before. Spotting a police car probably prompts you to put your foot on the brake and slow down (even if you weren't speeding). But when the police car is out of sight, your speed increases again. If you get fined, you probably won't speed for a while. But you will eventually speed again. The need to follow that rule hasn't been internalised. You only follow the rules when the 'punisher' (police officer) is there. The same is true for our kids. They will avoid the behaviour while you (the 'punisher') are there, but if they only stop to avoid the punishment, they will do it when you aren't there.

Children Need Discipline Not Punishment

So, should we let kids do whatever they want? Absolutely not. Children need guidance and direction. They need to be taught what is right and wrong. But they don't need to be hurt in the process. Punishment and discipline have too often been used as interchangeable terms, but the reality is they are polar opposites. Punishment is causing deliberate harm as retribution. In other words, making something bad happen to someone to make them 'pay' for what they did. Discipline, however, is teaching and directing your child to understand and take responsibility for their actions.

There has been much research to prove that punishment isn't effective in the long term (Markham, 2012). From the studies, some key reasons have been identified as to why punishment just doesn't seem to bring long-term change.

59

Why Doesn't Punishment Work?

- When we punish a child, they focus on what is happening to them rather than what they did wrong in the first place. They become more selfish and don't develop empathy for others.
- Punishment actually encourages children to lie to avoid future punishment rather than prevent the behaviour you are trying to stop.
- To make punishments work over a long period, their severity must be gradually increased. Parents often have a list of punishments they use to regulate their child's behaviour. However, what works for a while often becomes ineffective, and the severity of the threat must increase to have the same effect.
- Punishment makes the child feel bad about themselves rather than about the thing they did. If a child sees themselves as a 'bad' person, it makes sense that they will do 'bad' things.
- Children don't learn to take responsibility for their behaviour through punishment. They tend to believe their actions were driven by someone else, and blame others for what they did. This also means they end up thinking they need a parent to control behaviour.
- Punishment doesn't address what was behind the behaviour in the first place. It doesn't help the child learn to express their emotions. It squashes their needs and sends the message that their feelings aren't important.
- Punishment, even timeouts and taking away privileges, damages our relationship with our child. When children feel disconnected from their parents, their motivation to please them disappears.

How Discipline Works

Set Limits and Explain Them

Of course, you need to have rules. We want our kids to grow into adults that share our values, so make your expectations clear and explain why you have them. A child is more likely to follow a rule if they understand why it exists. For example, with household chores, you can explain that all members of the family help each other by doing different jobs. Emptying the dishwasher might be theirs. You should also acknowledge their perspective. When kids feel understood, they're more likely to accept our limits.

Understand that it is difficult to follow the rules sometimes. If possible, give your child a choice or redirect them toward what they CAN do to meet their needs or solve their problem. For example, "You wish you could play longer. It's hard to stop playing and have a bath. Would you like to put the bubble bath in?"

Allow Natural and Logical Consequences

Most of the time, if you talk through with your child what needs to happen, why it's important, and coach them with their response, a consequence isn't even necessary. However, there are times that consequences are a part of life (for all of us) and a way to help teach children the right things to do. In these situations, whenever possible, let your child feel the consequences of their behaviour (so long as it is not dangerous) and work with them to fix what they did wrong. A natural consequences is what would happen if nobody stepped in, for example if they refuse to wear a jumper, they will be cold. A logical consequence is enforced by the parent, but it makes sense with what has happened. For example, if they make a mess, they need to help clean it up. It wouldn't make sense to send them to bed early for making a mess. That consequence isn't connected to the behaviour, and it just causes confusion. Having logical consequences meaningfully links the child's behaviour to the broken rule. Logical consequences also need to be respectful, not yelling or causing shame, and reasonable for their age and ability (Nelson, 1985). Remember, the goal is to teach, not to punish.

Build on the Child/Parent Relationship

One of the most powerful influences you have on your child is your relationship with them. When trying to teach (discipline) your children, do it so they learn and grow, not to cause harm. When disciplining, sit with them, explain what rules were broken and what happened (consequences), and problem-solve solutions to help them rectify the situation. Doing this, we work together as a team without an 'us and them' mentality. We show understanding of how they felt and talk about how we, or others in the situation, felt. By acknowledging everyone's feelings, we connect with them and build understanding.

Ultimately, parents try their best to help their children grow and develop into 'good' people. Unfortunately, many of us were raised in a world where punishment was the main way to control behaviour.

61

The problem is, if we really want our kids to develop a moral conscience and take responsibility for their actions, punishment simply won't work.

We need to discipline our kids in the true sense of the word; we must teach, direct, and guide them. Working with them, rather than being an authority and causing fear, will help them develop at least the same moral standards as we do.

Children are supposed to get upset when they are overwhelmed. It doesn't make them bad and it doesn't make you a bad parent

@The_Therapist_Parent

True Discipline - Deep Dive Questions

If we want to teach our children and discipline them in the true sense of the word, then we have to find the most effective way for them to learn, not just follow what we say without question. In order to do this, we need to have boundaries, let our children experience the consequence of their choices, and support them.

1. Be Clear about Rules and Values

Think about the sort of person you hope your child will grow up to be. If you imagine them as an adult, how will they behave? What values will they have?

How are you teaching these values with your current rules?

Are there any rules you want to change or let go of? (e.g., do as they are told without question.)

2. Consequences

When your child breaks a rule or needs to learn a new way to do something, whenever possible, let your child feel the consequences of their behaviour (so long as it is not dangerous) and work with them to fix what they did wrong. Natural consequences occur without the parent needing to impose a consequence. Often, allowing the natural consequence will prevent a power struggle and the child will still learn the right lesson. Logical consequences involve action taken by the parent but the outcome fits the situation. For example, if they refuse to wear their helmet, they can't ride their bike. No consequence should ever place a child at risk for injury.

Here are some examples of natural and logical consequences. You can also add your own:

Situation	Natural Consequence
Child refuses to wear their jumper	They can experience the cold
They refuse to do their homework	They have to tell their teacher

Situation	Logical consequence
Makes a mess	They help clean it up
Damage something	They need to help fix it or earn money to go towards a new one (this is for older kids)
They hurt someone's feelings	They need to think of a way to fix the relationship

3. Work Together

When disciplining (teaching), find a time when you can both be calm. Sit with them, explain what happened and why it was a problem. Try and be empathetic, there could have been a reason why they did what they did, and we all make mistakes. Show understanding of how they felt and talk about how we, or others in the situation, felt. By acknowledging everyone's feelings, we connect with them and build understanding. Talk to them respectfully and involve them in the process. They need to be part of the solution, so problem-solve solutions together. When you work together, it takes away the 'us and them' mentality.

How to Stop Yelling and Avoid Power Struggles

We have all yelled at our kids at some point. I don't care if you are a psychologist, therapist, or a 'parenting expert,' we are all human, and kids have a way of pushing our buttons like no other; a battle of wills with a fight to the finish. The problem is nobody really wins. When our kids meet us with defiance and a you're-not-the-boss-of-me attitude, it can be like a red flag to a bull. We surge with emotion and are ready for battle. The problem is, this battle has more to do with us than our child. While yelling may work in the short term, in the long term, children will learn to block out the noise and, ultimately, block us out too.

Emotions are contagious. When we are stressed and angry, our kids will mirror the level of emotion we express. If we are triggered, our responses might be totally unreasonable for the situation, and we find we can't parent the way we'd prefer. Our emotions can escalate quickly and our kids will come along, meeting us at every level. If we want to stop yelling, we must look at ourselves and change our patterns.

Know Your Triggers

It would appear that a trigger happens automatically, and the reaction can seem totally justified at the time. But if we sit back and look at the situation when we are calm, it might be evident that our reaction was uncalled for. There is often another emotion underlying anger. Your child's behaviour might take you back to difficult times in your childhood or to how you were parented. It could also trigger fears about your parenting abilities or generate feelings of helplessness. In this way, our reaction to our child's behaviour has more to do with our difficulty processing such emotions than it does with the behaviour itself.

It may seem unlikely that emotions you felt as a child would come out as an adult. We may think that, surely, we have moved on from old wounds. But as an example, let's say when you were a child, you could not question your parent's authority without getting 'in trouble.'

So, when your child argues, this triggers you to rise up against their 'disobedience.' When, really, it is perfectly normal for a child to question or say "No" to their parents. Other common triggers might occur when your child cries, whines, or has a tantrum. Such behaviour often triggers people who, as children, were not allowed to express difficult emotions. The result is, we generally try to stop the behaviour by removing the child or becoming angry enough to shut them down.

To find our triggers, we need to become aware of our reactions. When we look honestly at our thoughts and feelings about these situations, we might be surprised at how unrealistic they are. That's because our outburst was an automatic response, and we couldn't think it through logically at the time.

Common thoughts behind triggers could be:
- You don't respect me.
- This is not convenient.
- I don't know what to do.
- I can't cope.
- I feel unappreciated.
- I want you to act like an adult.
- I can't do what I want to do.
- I am doing too much; I can't help you too.
- You are acting like my ex-partner.

Usually, when you can think about and admit that you have these thoughts, you realise that it is the thoughts, not your child's behaviour that makes you reactive. Giving yourself this grace allows you to recognise that your child's questioning or refusal doesn't necessarily mean they don't respect you.

Avoid Power Struggles

As adults, we can forget that children are people too. Just like us, children don't like to feel manipulated and powerless. When children start to say "No," developmentally, they are gaining independence and realising they have some choices. This is a positive stage in development, although it certainly doesn't feel like it at times. If we can take a moment to recognise that our children are seeking a level of control in their lives, we will see that it is unhelpful to take it away.

66

This doesn't mean just giving in to them but allowing them some choice. You can provide two options you are happy with. Then let your child to choose between those options rather than rebelling against your original request. This way, the child is still doing what you want, but they feel they have some control.

Is It Worth the Fight?

There are some situations where it really isn't worth the fight. In these situations, let your child live with the natural consequence of their choice. If your child wants to wear a thick coat in the middle of summer, let them experience the heat. This way, they learn for themselves, and you don't need to yell. Obviously, you can't do this if the consequence is dangerous, but if it is just discomfort, then let them decide. Experience teaches far more rapidly than words alone.

It's Normal, Not Personal

Too often, our expectations of what children can do are just not realistic for their level of maturity. Children's brains are still developing and will continue to do so into their 20s. They find transitions difficult; verbal instructions can be hard to process; and they have trouble expressing their needs. Some behaviour we find incredibly frustrating is actually completely normal. Children often don't have enough impulse control to stop doing what you told them not to do. A child usually won't go out of their way to upset us. Most of the time, they just respond the best way they know how, even if they say or do hurtful things.

Not many people can think clearly when they are upset, and children find this even harder because the logical thinking part of their brain is underdeveloped. It is important to remember that they are communicating how they feel, not making a judgment about you. If they have said hurtful things, you can discuss this once everyone is calm, rather than when emotions are escalated.

Meet Your Own Needs

I'm sure you have heard the saying, "You can't pour from an empty cup." Although most of us know this, we tend to dismiss it because there is usually just too much to be done. But you can't parent how you want to if your needs aren't being met.

You have to ensure you get enough sleep, eat well, see friends and maintain connections.

67

You need to ensure you have the opportunity to do things that you enjoy (and need) to make sure you are okay. Now, I know it is hard to make time when you have little children. But life has seasons. You may not be able to do an art class or something that takes you away from your children for long periods, but you can try and meet the basics, like eating a proper lunch and not just your child's scraps.

In the Moment

Everything we have discussed above is something we can do ahead of time. Each strategy certainly creates a positive foundation, but it won't necessarily remove the urge to yell in the moment. If yelling has been your first response and has developed into a habit, it will still be. Once you have recognised this, you can retrain yourself to do things differently. This won't happen instantly, so don't be too hard on yourself. It takes time and a conscious effort to stop right when you are triggered. In that moment, you can tell your children, "I can feel that I'm getting angry, and I don't want to yell, so I'm going to take a break till I can speak calmly." There is nothing wrong with putting yourself in 'time out' if needed. In fact, it is a great way to teach your kids that we all need to take time to maintain or regain a sense of calm. If you do start yelling, try to stop in the middle of it. Take a breath and start again. Say, "I need a do-over. I don't want to yell, so I'm going to try again." This is also an amazing way to demonstrate to our children that we can all struggle with emotions. Still, we can learn to regulate them – and support each other in the process.

Repair Together

If you have yelled or reacted in a way you wish you hadn't, you need to own your part of the situation and apologise to your child. This will actually help your relationship, so it's not such a battle. If you and your child are butting heads regularly over the same issue, then it is important to work through it together. Involving them to come up with ideas of what you both can do differently will help them feel valued. Be sure to really listen to how they feel and don't try and justify your behaviour when you yell or go too far. You are responsible for your feelings. They didn't 'make you frustrated,' they may have done something that triggered you, but it was your trigger that caused the reaction.

Changing the habit of yelling takes practice and patience. It involves self-reflection and the ability to challenge our beliefs. Still, like anything, the more we hone this skill, the easier it will become to recognise and respond to, rather than react to, our triggers. The important thing is to not be too hard on yourself. We are all human, and it is going to happen. Just as long as we recognise an outburst for what it really is and are open enough to repair damaged relationships when needed.

Why we yell....

Unresolved trauma

Our unmet needs

Needing support

Sensory overload

Our expectations are too high

@The_Therapist_Parent

Identifying Your Triggers - Deep Dive Questions

Even if we have the intention to respond in a connected way to our children, nobody can do it all the time. What gets in the way of being able to connect? The following can contribute:

- Lack of sleep.
- Thinking you will reinforce 'bad behaviour.'
- Expecting too much of your child.
- feeling judged by those around you.
- Feeling overwhelmed or busy.

What else would you add to the list? Think about a time your child was upset and your response left you feeling disconnected from each other (and probably more upset). Write about what your difficulties were.

Now, let's take time to work out your triggers. Write about what happens before you are triggered; what really pushes you to react? How does your body feel when your child has an emotional meltdown? What are your thoughts during the emotional explosion? How do you feel after the wave has passed? Are you more logical or emotional in how you respond?

What else influences your triggers?

Let's work out where your triggers came from. When you were a child, how did your family manage feelings? Were your emotions dismissed or shamed by your parents so you learned to shut down or ignore them? Or, did emotions always seem to be big, so you felt the need to protect yourself? What did or didn't work when it came to emotions in your family?

What do you want to keep and what do you want to change?

Being aware is helpful in bringing about change, but remember it takes practise to consciously alter the way we respond when we are triggered. We have been wired to respond that way, and it takes time to re-wire, but it can be done.

Our reactions have more to do with (our triggers) than they do our children's behaviour

It's up to us to look at what's going on behind our (own) behaviours

@The_Therapist_Parent

Avoiding Power Struggles - Deep Dive Questions

1. It Starts with Me

We are always modelling behaviour to our children. Have you ever heard your child snap back at you in a harsh tone and thought, is that how I sound? Like it or not, children are going to learn how to behave during conflict and high emotions from us. Have a think about your body language, tone of voice, and what you say when you are frustrated and angry. What would you like to change?

2. Rather than Say "No," Have Them Work Through It

If a child asks to do something and you can't for whatever reason, it is easy just to say, "No, we can't. There is too much on," (or whatever fits your circumstance). A child will react with disappointment and often push back. Instead, see if they can come to the conclusion themselves. You can't expect young children to do this without support, but it is a good opportunity for children to practise problem-solving. You could say, "That would be great. We have to do (add reason here). Do you think we could fit that in, too?" As they come up with ideas, work through whether those things are possible. Your child may still feel frustrated, but it won't be as much of a power struggle. Think of times when you could have done this.

3. Say "Yes" Where You Can

Parents don't usually like saying "No" to their kids all the time, but we can't do everything and we have to use our judgement to keep our kids safe. However, when our child asks for something, there is often something we can say "Yes" to. If they ask to go to the park but haven't finished their chores, you could say, "Yes, as soon as you have finished." Often it is the initial "No" they hear that causes the push back. Think of times when you could have said "Yes" to a part or all of a request, but still fitted the situation into your boundaries.

4. Pick Your Battles

Some battles just aren't worth fighting. These are the ones that you leave to natural consequences or you just let go. Sometimes, they only become a battle because we are worried about what others think if our child turns up wearing a tutu and gumboots, for example. But when we remove our feelings about others judging us, does it really matter? If the answer is "No," then let it go. What are some battles you can let go of?

Attention Seeking Should Not Be Ignored

Often, over the years, I have heard people shut down any reaction to a child's unfavourable behaviour, saying, "They are just attention seeking. Ignore them." But when did 'attention seeking' become a 'bad' thing? Yes, children often choose the most annoying ways to seek our attention, but the need for attention isn't bad. The need for attention is the most normal and natural thing for a child to experience. Gaining attention and attaching to an adult is a primal instinct; yet, when a child does this in an unfavourable way, we ignore it. The problem is, ignoring a child's attention-seeking behaviour doesn't stop their need. In fact, ignoring a child's need for attention usually means that they will become more desperate for attention, and their behaviour will escalate. They will do what they have to until they get the attention they are looking for. This isn't always positive attention, but it is still attention.

A child's most well-developed form of communication is behaviour. You can't expect that a three-year-old will say, "I am very angry you gave me the wrong coloured cup. I would like you to get the blue one. Also, I'm having trouble calming myself down, so could I have a hug?" I know that sounds ridiculous. Not even an adult would articulate their needs like that, but so often, this seems to be the expectation adults have of children. The truth is children's brains are still forming. They will naturally end up in the emotional/non-logical part of their brain because that is what is developing. They are often overwhelmed by emotions and trying to work them all out. They also won't have the vocabulary to express what they are feeling. So, what is left? Behaviour. Sometimes children (and adults) don't even know what they want. They just know they don't feel right. So, when a child's behaviour is attention-seeking, it is our job to help them find the need behind the behaviour and coach them through meeting it.

What Is Attention-Seeking Behaviour?

Attention-seeking behaviour is any behaviour your child engages in that causes you to give them your full attention. Usually, when we think of this type of behaviour, it is the really challenging or annoying actions.

74

Such as, how your child, who has not really seemed to want your attention all day, suddenly starts yelling or climbing on the furniture as soon as you use your phone. Or, it is the grating tone in their voice as they whine, "It's not fair!" For others, it could be the meltdown in the supermarket in front of a host of judging eyes. These are all attention-seeking behaviours. The child is speaking a need through their behaviour. However, there are other attention-seeking behaviours that people don't often consider.

- Pretending to be sick or exaggerating a sickness or injury.
- Being 'over dramatic' in any situation.
- Always wanting to be the leader and putting themselves first (normal for young children).
- Seeking praise and always talking about what they have done well.
- Lying about achievements and abilities.
- Hurting siblings.
- Doing anything, however annoying, to get your attention.

Any of these behaviours are attention-seeking. They are different behaviours because they communicate different needs, but they all require attention to help meet those needs.

We must look past the behaviour and find what that need might be. For a child who is exaggerating injuries, they may feel that they need more nurturing. A child who is 'over-dramatic' may feel that they are often overlooked in the family. A child who puts themselves first might feel that they are only important if they are first. When children seem to fish for praise, or lie about their abilities, it could mean that they have low self-esteem. A child who is hurting siblings or constantly doing something to upset you might be getting bullied, have a new sibling, or feel bad for another reason which comes out in them wanting to make others feel bad too. Children don't necessarily enjoy attention-seeking behaviour. They do it because they need help, and the only way they can get that help is with your attention.

What Can You Do When Your Child Is 'Attention Seeking?'

It might seem simple and at times completely against what you want to do, but when your child is 'attention seeking,' you need to give them your attention. That doesn't mean you just allow the problematic behaviours to continue, but you don't ignore them either. Remember, ignoring the behaviour will only make them feel like they need to turn up the volume to be heard. In giving our kids the attention they need, we also want them to learn how to recognise their needs and express them in a more favourable way. Children will only learn this if we teach them.

1.Label the Feeling and the Need for Your Child:

Saying things like, "You seem really frustrated," "You really want my attention right now," "You seem to need a lot of cuddles at the moment," or "It feels good to be first," can help a child better recognise the need or feeling behind their behaviour. Make sure you are willing to be corrected by your child. You may get the feeling or need wrong. That's okay, but make sure you have your child try to explain what they think is going on. As you do this, your child will start to feel understood. Just feeling that a parent sees their perspective will greatly impact the child. When we do this, we are also helping our children to recognise what is happening so, as their brain develops, they can make this connection without having to jump straight to a behaviour to communicate for them.

2.Use Empathy:

When we empathise with our children, we build connection. If we can say, "I feel like that sometimes too," or, "I think I would be upset if that happened to me," we show them that they are not alone. We understand that dealing with emotions can be hard. We stop there from being sides of 'us and them' and we join together in understanding.

3.Offer Direction If You Can:

It is a great skill to teach your kids to express when they feel like they need more of your attention. Until they can, though, you will have to do this for them. If they aren't too upset by the situation, you can try to offer a solution, such as, "It seems like you really want me to spend time with you and you don't like it when I have to make a phone call. I do need to make this call, but how about we play one game, and then I make the call?" This is a great strategy; however, it will only work if you can talk to them before their emotions have escalated too far.

76

4.What Could They Do Next Time?:

When everyone is calm, you can talk about what they could do if they experience a similar situation or feelings like that again. High emotions are not the time to try to problem-solve, so don't do it in the moment. But later, when you both feel calm, talk about what they could do.

5.Give Them Time:

All children need our attention. It is normal. Life can get very busy, and you can find that the only time you spend with your child is in the car on the way to the next activity or as you quickly brush their teeth before bed. Ultimately, the way to help reduce attention-seeking behaviour is to spend time with your children. This can be hard when you are busy with work, life, and other children, but it doesn't have to be for long periods. It is better to have 10-minute blocks consistently, where you play a game with them or sit and have a conversation, than long periods of time only every now and then. Try to set a special routine for each child, even if it is cuddles and a story at bedtime; some consistent one-on-one time will work wonders.

Attention is a primal need that every child will seek to have met. If a child is 'attention seeking,' then they have a need to communicate to you through their behaviour, and they need your attention to help meet it. As we meet our kid's needs and redirect them if they ask in unfavourable ways, we teach them how to get and give positive attention, something that is required for all healthy relationships.

All behaviour is communication. If we get caught up in how the communication is delivered, instead of the need behind it, a child will (turn up) the volume to be heard, or shut down the need completely .

@The_Therapist_Parent

Attention Seeking - Deep Dive Questions

What are the behaviours your child engages in that get your attention? What are the things you just can't ignore?

- Pretending to be sick/injured or exaggerating.
- Being 'over dramatic' in any situation.
- Always wanting to be the leader and putting themselves first (normal for young children).
- Seeking praise and always talking about what they have done well.
- Lying about achievements and abilities.
- Hurting siblings.
- Whining.
- Yelling, screaming, etc.
- Interrupting.

Can you think of more?

It is key is to not focus on the behaviour but what is behind the behaviour. What do you think is behind your child's behaviour?

- Are they seeking more nurturing?
- Do they feel overlooked in the family?
- Are they trying to feel important?
- Do they have low self-esteem?
- Are they being bullied?
- Are they struggling to cope with a big change?
- Are they just feeling like they need more attention?

Can you think of more?

They do it because they need help, and the only way they can get that help is with your attention.

When you have worked out what could be behind the behaviour, you can make a plan to address the need. If they need more time with you, can you make a plan to have 10 minutes of uninterrupted and intentional time with them each day? If they are struggling with their self-esteem, what could you do to build this up? (You will find some ideas for this in *How to Build Your Child's Self-Esteem* on page 229.)

What plan could you make to meet your child's need?

When Anger Turns Aggressive

When children are emotionally dysregulated, it can be exhausting for everyone. Occasionally, these challenges escalate into aggressive behaviour, raising safety concerns. These outbursts generally stem from children grappling with intense emotions beyond their maturity level. It's important to note that these outbursts don't indicate a bad child or parent; instead, they highlight the child's limited brain development and emotional management skills.

When a child is completely overwhelmed by their emotions, two parts of the brain come into play: the amygdala and the hypothalamus. The amygdala, resembling an almond in shape, is linked to emotions like anger and fear. Meanwhile, the hypothalamus, located at the base of the brain, handles survival functions such as temperature and heart rate regulation. An apt analogy for understanding emotional meltdown is to imagine the amygdala as the brain's smoke detector and the hypothalamus as the decision-maker determining whether to put water (calming strategies) or gasoline (hormones) on the fire (Fields, 2016).

The prefrontal cortex is the part of the brain that helps us think through a situation before we react. When it comes to emotional meltdowns, Dr Mary Gleason (2020) describes this as a pot of boiling water, with the prefrontal cortex as a lid. When a child is in meltdown, the intensity of the feelings overwhelm their ability to make sense of it, causing the feelings to become stronger than the lid.

Various factors can trigger a child's aggressive outbursts, including immaturity, anxiety, ADHD, and poor impulse control. Undiagnosed learning disorders can cause children to explode in frustration. While other children might struggle with unexpected changes or sensory processing difficulties. Regardless of the specific cause, the outcome results from immature brain development and the lack of appropriate skills to manage overwhelming emotions. Until children have learned how to problem-solve, communicate their needs, and calm effectively, outbursts are likely to occur.

Unfortunately, meltdowns can become aggressive, posing risks to the child and those around them. It's not uncommon for children to lose control during these episodes, directing their anger at a parent through actions like screaming, throwing things, hitting, and biting. This is a scary and stressful experience for everyone, including the child.

Post-meltdown, after they've worn themselves out and calmed down, children often feel remorse. They don't enjoy the meltdown; they don't want to do it. At the time, they have lost all control and don't know what else to do. During such moments, their amygdala detects a threat (real or imagined,) triggering the hypothalamus into a survival mode that leads to an instinctual reaction. They may comprehend why their body reacts with tense muscles, a racing heart, sweaty hands, and a focus on physical actions like hitting and kicking. No matter what you say at this time, the child can't hear you. Their thinking and reasoning faculties have switched off, and they solely focus on survival.

What to Do When a Child Has a Meltdown?

All behaviour communicates a message. In this situation, the child is in distress. They aren't trying to manipulate you or deliberately harm you, even though it may feel like it. They are in survival mode, doing what they believe is necessary to navigate the situation.

Our response in these moments is crucial and can determine whether the situation escalates or calms. Over time, as children grow and experience our support, they will learn better emotional management strategies. The following steps can be beneficial when dealing with a child in meltdown.

1.Stay Calm: Staying calm can be one of the toughest aspects of parenting. Even when a child is screaming or saying hurtful things, we must remain composed. Responding with aggression will only escalate the situation, so we must be the ones to initiate calmness.

2.Ensure Safety: If your child becomes physically aggressive, promptly separate them from the situation to prevent harm. You cannot allow physical violence. Be explicitly clear that 'We don't hit.' Stay calm and be assertive without resorting to yelling or aggression while maintaining firm boundaries for safety.

3.Maintain Boundaries: Stay calm, kind, and empathetic without compromising your boundaries. If an escalation began because you said "No" to something, granting the request now won't benefit anyone. Do empathise with the child, though. Acknowledge their difficulty with hearing "No" or not getting what they want while keeping your boundary intact.

4.Help Them Calm: If they have escalated to the point of violence, they may not want a hug or to try calming activities. Maintain a close but non-intrusive presence, letting them know you are there to help if they need it, but don't pressure them. When they are ready, offer a hug or whatever calming support they need.

5.Plan for the Future: Eventually, discuss the incident, even if it is a couple of days later for older children. Avoid blame and judgment and instead express curiosity and empathy by acknowledging their feelings. These situations will likely recur, so work together to identify what they could do differently next time and what changes might be needed. Approach it as a collaborative effort, recognising that both you and your child may need to adjust your actions.

Violent outbursts in children are frightening for everyone involved, including the child. Time-outs and punishments aren't effective for teaching a child how to manage overwhelming feelings. Safety is vital, which may mean removing them or yourself from the situation, but isolation is not the answer. Once the outburst has subsided, discuss the feelings of the emotions and the coping and management strategies the child could use next time.

Before reacting, pause and look for what is behind the  anger

@The_Therapist_Parent

Anger Ladder Activity

There are many types of emotion charts. It doesn't matter if you use a thermometer of emotions, a ladder, a volcano, or a simple 0-10 scale of emotions. All of these charts are effective because they all have some very important things in common. They give the child the opportunity to identify an emotion without having to verbally express it. They help the child to label the emotion and explicitly show the increasing intensity of it.

Verbally expressing emotions can be difficult for anyone, but it is even more difficult for children. As a child's vocabulary is underdeveloped, they may not have the words to describe the difference between being frustrated and annoyed. However, they can point to a chart that visually represents this. If we create a visual chart which incorporates language around emotions, they begin to understand the difference between annoyed, upset, frustrated, angry and furious. If we link these with the physical cues they experience, we also teach the intensity of the emotion.

A thermometer is often used to represent the levels of anger. It is a good analogy as long as your child understands what a thermometer is. It does visually represent the changing nature of emotions effectively.

Having a numbered scale can also be helpful. By using numbers, children can easily tell you where they are sitting emotionally, without having to go into detail. Similarly, a parent can easily help their child by labelling the behaviour. For example, "Your voice is getting louder and you are frowning, I think you are a three."

I have drawn my version of the anger ladder. However, when you do this, I encourage you to involve your child as much as possible. Have them colour, choose pictures, or at least tell you where to put things.

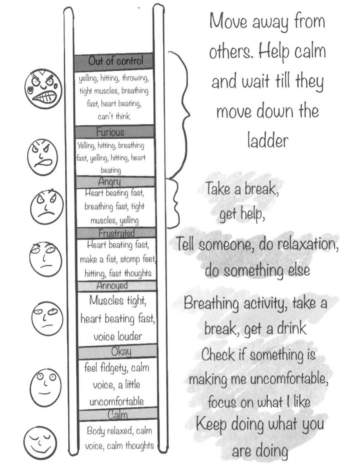

Out of control
yelling, hitting, throwing, tight muscles, breathing fast, heart beating, can't think

Furious
Yelling, hitting, breathing fast, yelling, hitting, heart beating

Angry
Heart beating fast, breathing fast, tight muscles, yelling

Frustrated
Heart beating fast, make a fist, stomp feet, hitting, fast thoughts

Annoyed
Muscles tight, heart beating fast, voice louder

Okay
feel fidgety, calm voice, a little uncomfortable

Calm
Body relaxed, calm voice, calm thoughts

Move away from others. Help calm and wait till they move down the ladder

Take a break, get help,

Tell someone, do relaxation, do something else

Breathing activity, take a break, get a drink

Check if something is making me uncomfortable, focus on what I like

Keep doing what you are doing

Have them think about what their body feels like at each step. What are some things they might be doing? What are their thoughts like?

At this point it is helpful to brainstorm with the child. What could they do to help calm as they go up the ladder? By doing this you give them a plan and allow them to see that they have choices with their anger. They don't have to get to the point of being out of control.

Anger Snowball Activity

The key to emotion regulation is to catch it early. This is easier said than done. It can be hard to teach children that there are 'levels' of an emotion; that each level of intensity has a different consequence and a different way to problem-solve.

So often, I have had children replay stories to me where something triggered their anger. This may have been something really insignificant (although not for them), such as not being able to have their favourite cereal for breakfast. Or it could be something more obvious, like being teased by another child. Either way, this trigger starts them on the path of becoming annoyed, frustrated, angry, enraged, and totally out of control.

Children aren't able to think logically about consequences when they are in an emotional state. Neither are adults for that matter. But adults have had more practice in experiencing the consequences, which makes this a little easier. For children, it is important that when they are calm, we talk them through what some alternatives may have been. Have them think of alternative scenarios that might have played out if they had been able to manage their anger earlier. In doing this, they are preparing themselves to see that they have some control. They don't have to be completely led by the emotion.

One Technique Is to Use the Anger Snowball

1. Work Backwards

No doubt you will have the end story already. You will already know about the fight, the things thrown, or whatever the end result was. What you want to do is go right back to the beginning. What was the initial trigger? What set the child off on this path?

Be curious. Make sure you keep asking, "Did anything else happen before that?" Eventually, you will get to the trigger.

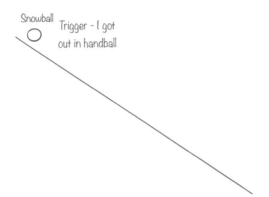

2. Then What Happened?

Keep asking what happened next. Make sure they don't just skip over the stages of the anger to the final outcome. We want to know each detail that built the anger to the explosion at the end.

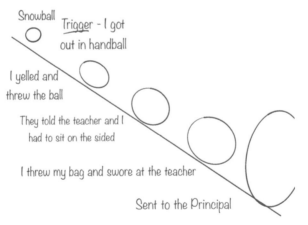

3. How Could It Be Different?

Make sure you point out how the anger built up. Be empathetic; nobody likes being angry. The child didn't want to be out of control, they just didn't know how or when to stop.

Start by saying, "What if we were able to stop the snowball before it got too big?" "What if we put a rock in to stop it from rolling down and getting bigger?"

This time start from the bottom up. Draw a rock at each snowball and discuss what would have happened if they were able to stop there. Work out what would be different? how would others around them be different?

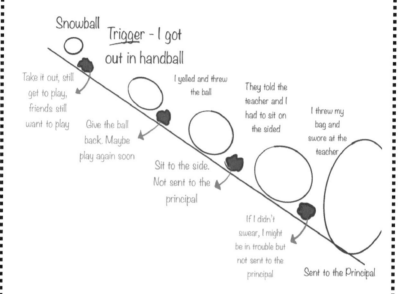

Snowball

Trigger - I got out in handball

Take it out, still get to play, friends still want to play

Give the ball back. Maybe play again soon

I yelled and threw the ball

They told the teacher and I had to sit on the sided

I threw my bag and swore at the teacher

Sit to the side. Not sent to the principal

If I didn't swear, I might be in trouble but not sent to the principal

Sent to the Principal

4. How Could We Stop It?

Now work out the different ways they would need to manage the level of anger at each rock. Strategies you would use when the snowball is small are going to be different from when the snowball is huge. Try to think of realistic strategies for the situation.

Jumping on a trampoline might be great to help a child retain their calm, but if they are at school, this may not be possible. You can also add some helpful thoughts they could have used at each stage. The repetition of strategies and thoughts will eventually make it easier for the child to choose these, even when they are in the middle of an emotional storm.

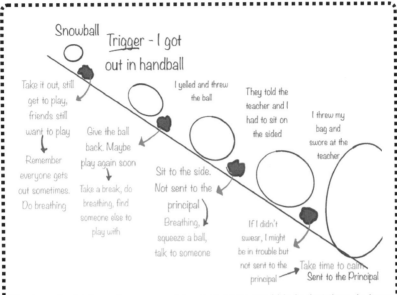

The important information we want to pass on to our kids is that they do have choices, they have alternatives, and they are capable of making changes. In doing this exercise with children, they learn to identify the stages of their anger and problem-solve alternatives at every stage.

What Kids Wished Their Parents Knew

I have spent the past 20 years talking to kids. During that time, I have heard a lot of the same themes. Often, kids don't feel like their parents understand them or what they go through each day. The problem is, kids don't tell their parents what they want or need from them. One reason for this is developmental. Children, especially young kids, find it difficult to see other people's perspectives. They assume you know what is going on in their head.

The other reason is that parents don't ask. Not many adults have the courage to tell other adults what they want them to do differently. So, imagine how difficult it is for a child to tell a parent that. For this to happen, there needs to be trust and an assurance that the parent will listen. This is not meant to make parents feel guilty. We all get busy with life, but it doesn't hurt to stop and reflect on how we interact with our children.

Most parents I have worked with want to do better and desire to improve their relationships with their children. But we must remember that it can't all be one way. If we want our children to listen to us, we must listen to them, too.

The following are some of the things children have shared with me that could make good conversation starters for parents.

"Sometimes when I say "No," I just don't agree. I'm not trying to be disrespectful."

As parents, we can become stuck in insisting our children obey without question. Sure, if they did, life might be easier. But do we really want our kids to obey mindlessly? Don't we want our kids to have an opinion and express it when they think something isn't right?

What we really want our kids to learn is that there is a respectful way to disagree. We need to remember this too. When our child argues, we can feel infuriated and dig our heels in. We tend to fight back with just as much conviction as they do because their disagreement feels like an attack on our authority. However, if we pause to consider whether our child intended to be disrespectful, we often discover that they were only expressing their opinion. From there, we can step back and focus on having a respectful conversation. Children need to experience a respectful disagreement if they are going to be able to express their opinion respectfully.

"Punishment doesn't work, it just makes me feel sad."

I hear this one a lot. Kids tell me that being grounded or sent to their room doesn't stop them from doing things wrong. What it does is make them feel bad about themselves, feeling like they always make mistakes. This doesn't mean that they think that they should be able to do whatever they want, they know that there have to be rules. Kids know there are consequences when they do the wrong thing, but it needs to make sense for them to learn to do things differently.

I recently asked some children about what does work when they do something they shouldn't. One child gave me an example of leaving food scraps in the family car. When the parents found out, the child was no longer allowed to eat in the car. It was a logical consequence of the action, and the child realised their mistake, explaining, "That worked. Grounding me wouldn't have done anything." It is interesting that what kids reveal is what research shows; logical and natural consequences work better than punishments. The consequence needs to fit the behaviour; otherwise, it can feel to the child like they are a victim and not responsible for what they did. Perhaps, we should have been listening to kids all along!

"I love them even when I'm angry with them."

Like anyone in the heat of the moment, children can lose their temper and say or do things they later regret. But kids have had less practise managing their emotions, so they will likely lose control more often. We mustn't take their comments personally. But once the feeling has passed and the child can think clearly again, everyone should feel confident that the relationship remains strong.

This doesn't mean that children can use their parents as punching bags just because they are angry. You can talk about how their words hurt you, but they also need to know that your love is still there, and you know they love you, too. Likewise, they need to know that you will still love them, no matter how unlovable they may act. There needs to be reassurance that anger does not negate love.

"I want them to spend time with me. Just me."

It is easy for kids to feel invisible. Parents get busy with work, chores, and managing the family as a whole. At school, they are just another face in a sea of children. As much as they might hear their parents say they are special, or even how good they are, it doesn't impact them if they don't feel seen. Sometimes, we think that because our kids are with us a lot, we are spending time with them. But taking them places, or even being in the same house, doesn't mean you are spending time together.

Now, spending time doesn't have to involve hours of undivided attention to have an impact. It can be a lot of small moments. A wink, a rub on the back, or an 'in joke.' There are many ways you can make small connections each day. However, there still needs to be some child-led one-on-one time. Whether it is stories in bed or a board game, it is in these moments that you build a space where your child feels important, safe, and connected. With a strong foundation here, children will feel comfortable talking to you and sharing their lives.

"I want them to be happy with me."

Most parents' response to this one is either, "Of course I'm happy with you," or "I would be happier with you if you did what you were asked." However, both of these responses miss the point. Kids want to feel that you are happy they came into your life. They want to know they aren't a burden but that you delight in them. Although most of us adore our kids, we don't show it as often as we could. If we take moments to laugh with our kids, enjoy their uniqueness, and express how we appreciate them, we allow them to see what a gift they really are.

"I want to do some things for myself."

It can be hard to let our kids do things for themselves. It can definitely be frustrating and time-consuming to have them learn on their own, but it is essential we give them some freedom to try. Allowing kids independence helps them develop necessary skills and builds confidence. Kids learn that you trust them and will help them if they make mistakes. We need to be a safe place from which they can explore and develop their competence.

These are just a few inner thoughts children have shared over the years. There are plenty more, and each child has their own list of wishes. However, kids won't just come out and tell you these thoughts. You must be a safe place for them and express your curiosity for them to share. If we stay tuned in to our kids, we should get clues as to what they really need us to know. Asking our kids what they wish we knew or what we could do differently as parents doesn't put them in charge. It just gives us insight into what they need.

A child saying "no" doesn't mean they are being disrespectful. We need to teach children how to have respectful disagreements

@The_Therapist_Parent

What Do Your Kids Wish You Knew?

No parent is perfect, and every child has different needs. What will help one child, may not be helpful for another. Parents can feel lost with what to do and forget that it could help to simply ask their child. Children may not have the vocabulary to explain everything, and their needs will change as they get older, but it is a wonderful practice to check in with your child about your parenting. They will give you insight that you won't get from any book or blog.

Parents often feel strange asking their children about how they are parenting because they don't like to seem vulnerable or as if they are giving their children power over them. This isn't about power. It's not about changing rules and a child thinking they can dictate. It is about trying to be the best parent you can be for the child you have.

I encourage you to sit with your child and ask these questions. Try not to get defensive, you want to have an idea of what things are like from their perspective. If you hate doing something and it isn't working, you need to know why.

What do you like/dislike about being in our family?

If you could change anything about our family, what would it be?

Be careful to listen to what is really behind the answer. They may say they wish their brother wasn't born, or something similar. But what are they really saying? Is it, I want more time with you? Be curious, not judgemental.

What are the things that I do that you like?

Is there anything you think I could do better as a parent?

Is there anything I can help you with?

Do you feel like I understand you?

Now reflect on those answers. What did you learn about your child? What changes do you think you will make?

Why Parents Need to Say Sorry

We want our children to be respectful of others' feelings and quick to admit when they are wrong. We want them to give a sincere apology and learn from their mistakes. But how many parents apologise to their children?

We live in a culture where it is usual for adults to feel superior to children. Adults with this belief, therefore, don't feel they owe a child an apology, even when they are in the wrong. Parents may worry that admitting wrongdoing to a child will undermine their authority. Or they feel justified in their actions because the child drove them to behave that way, so they have no need apologise. Each of these beliefs is false and can damage our relationships with our kids. It also means our children miss out on the lessons they could learn from our apologies.

The Benefits of Apologising to Our Children

Although parents can feel vulnerable when they apologise to their kids, the benefits can be life-changing. You may notice the following things when you make apologising a standard practice in your household.

Improved Relationships: Parents fear their children won't respect them if they admit they are wrong. But the truth is, children respect this willingness. A sincere apology actually strengthens the bond between a parent and a child. When you apologise you acknowledge your child's feelings, showing they are important to you. Your apology shows you realise your relationship has been damaged and want to repair it. Asking your child to forgive you doesn't give them power over you, but it does show you value them enough to appreciate their forgiveness. This vulnerability and acceptance in your relationship demonstrate to your child that you care, and this strengthens your bond.

Acceptance of Mistakes: When we admit we get it wrong sometimes, we allow our children the freedom to make mistakes. If kids think adults don't make mistakes, they will ultimately have unrealistic expectations of themselves. By involving them with apologies, we show that making mistakes is inevitable. And when we admit what we have done, we have opportunities to learn and move on.

97

Modelling: There is no better place for a child to learn than from their parents. But if a child never sees or experiences the benefit of an apology, how will they know to do this themselves? A sincere apology, rather than a quick "Sorry," will help children navigate relationships for the rest of their lives. When they see your bravery and willingness to be vulnerable, they will learn to have the courage to do this for themselves.

Accountability: When we apologise to our children, we teach them that we are each responsible for our own actions. No matter what drove us to do or say what we did, apologising for our part shows that we had a choice, and we chose the wrong one. By doing this, we teach our children that they are accountable for their choices; and we can't use others as an excuse for our behaviour.

Learning Experiences: When parents apologise to their children, they draw a clear line around what behaviour is okay and what isn't. You can talk to your child about what you should do next time and even problem-solve together about what to do in a similar situation to ensure you don't make the same mistakes.

How We Get It Wrong

Sorry but…: Often, parents think they have apologised to their children, but they have begun with, "I'm sorry, but…" When we add the "but," we contradict the apology. This addition means we feel we were justified in our behaviour, e.g., "I'm sorry I yelled, but you wouldn't hurry up, and we were late." That isn't an apology. It's a justification. This is not to make parents feel guilty. We have all yelled when we are stressed. That is reality. We are human, and we make mistakes. However, this is even more reason to explain our part in the problem.

Poor Timing: We may realise we have said or done the wrong thing, but if we yell, "I'm sorry," it will lose meaning. Wait until you are calm enough to talk with a kind and sincere tone. That way, your child won't be defensive and feel they need to fight back.

Bring Up Past Wrongs: When apologising for your actions, leave it at that. Don't bring up times your child has done the wrong thing. If the conversation leads to them recognising what they did wrong, that's great; talk about it, but don't point it out in your apology.

What to Do Instead

When we apologise to our kids, we need to focus on our actions and what we did that wasn't appropriate. We need to be sincere and make it clear that we are genuine. Take the time to sit with them, use a calm voice, and look them in the eye (if they are comfortable with this.) Recognise how you both felt and plan what you can do next time. Imagine you've yelled at your child as you rush out the door because you are running late (and who hasn't?) You could say, "I'm sorry I yelled at you to hurry up. I was stressed because we were running late. But I shouldn't have yelled at you." You could ask them how they felt and recognise that it wasn't fun for anyone. Then problem-solve together to avoid repeating the situation.

Taking the time to apologise to your children will strengthen your relationship, help them feel valued, and model appropriate behaviour that will enhance their relationships throughout their lives.

When we admit to our children that we are wrong sometimes, we give them the freedom to make mistakes

@The_Therapist_Parent

How to Apologise - Deep Dive Questions

When we apologise to our kids, we need to focus on our actions and what we did that wasn't appropriate. Don't make this about what they did that may have triggered it all, keep it about what you did. Don't rush an apology, take the time to sit with them, use a calm voice, and look them in the eye (if they are comfortable with this). Recognise how you both felt and plan what you can do next time.

Think of a time when your behaviour wasn't at it's best. What, specifically, was it that you did?

How were you both feeling?

If your friend or partner had done the same to you, how would you want them to apologise? Think of the tone of voice, facial expression, and body language you would expect them to use.

Do you have any fears about apologising to your child? What will the outcome be?

Should We Force Children to Apologise?

There is much controversy around whether parents should make their children apologise when they do something wrong. One school of thought says children don't develop a 'theory of mind' and an understanding of other's perspectives until five years of age. Therefore, they cannot really understand what they are doing when they say sorry. The belief behind this outlook is that if you force a child to say sorry, you teach them to lie since they don't have the empathy necessary to feel sorry.

Another school of thought says children from the age of 18 months do have some understanding of other people's feelings, especially if they are upset. Therefore, children would be able to understand the impact of an apology.

However, empathy is more complicated than that, and teaching children to mend relationships involves more than just saying sorry.

According to Dr Erin Leonard in *Psychology Today* (Jul 2018), there are three types of empathy:
1. Emotional Sharing: we feel distressed when we see others distressed.
2. Empathic Concern: we want to help.
3. Perspective Taking: we can imagine what it is like to be the other person.

When we look at empathy in this way, it becomes apparent that it doesn't fully develop at one age. Understanding grows in complexity over time. So, while true prospective taking doesn't really develop until a child is around the age of five–seven years, an understanding of emotions (in oneself and others) can be taught much earlier than this. Despite the controversy, one thing is clear, to truly apologise, there must be empathy.

How to Build Empathy

When complex emotions come up for our children, we need to be able to 'emotion coach' them through their feelings. Specific steps need to be taken when we 'emotion coach.'

1. Acknowledge the Emotion: Whatever the situation, if you want to connect with your child and help them, you must start by acknowledging their feelings. If your child is upset, the 'thinking' part of their brain is switched off. They are in their 'emotional brain.' So, if you say, "Why did you do that?" or, "Don't be scared," they will be reactive, not logical. The only way to help your child move out of this emotional state is to meet them in the emotion and label it. You can say, "You must be very angry right now," or "Yes, it can be scary."

2. Use Empathy and Listen to Their Perspective: Parents can struggle with this, as the desire is usually to jump in and fix the problem. We tend to be better at sympathy than empathy. Sympathy recognises the emotion but wants to fix it quickly. That's when we try to see the silver lining. In these situations, we might say, "At least you tried your best." Although we might mean to focus on the positives of the situation, what this actually does is minimises the child's feelings, which can ultimately disconnect the relationship. If we are to teach our kids empathy, we must show them empathy. We need to sit in that emotion and just say, "I get it." When they feel heard, they will calm, and you can move on to the next stage.

3. Problem-Solve Together: When your child feels calm and heard, then, and only then, will they be able to access their 'thinking brain.' When they can think clearly, they will have the best chance of understanding how others feel. This is the start of understanding the need to apologise and mend relationships. While in this mode, you can talk them through how the other person may feel. Try to get them to work it out for themselves, but support them if they need help. Then talk about what they could do to help the other person feel better and how the relationship could be mended.

If we prioritise building empathy, there will be many other benefits. Our children will start to recognise their own emotions and regulate themselves more easily. They will build problem-solving skills and see situations from others' perspectives. In addition, as we act as 'emotion coach,' we improve our connection and relationship with our children.

To Apologise or Not to Apologise

So, do we force children to apologise? I would suggest not. But should we encourage an apology? Yes, definitely. If we force children to say sorry when they are in the heat of the moment, it is doubtful they will offer a genuine apology. Remember, they can't access their 'thinking brain,' so they are unable to see how the other person feels. Chances are, they feel quite justified with what has happened and not sorry at all. That is why 'emotion coaching' them first is essential. We need to move them out of their emotionally reactive state by empathising with them.

Discuss how others may have felt once they are ready to talk about what happened. Ask what they want to happen; what they might do to fix the situation. But don't expect that children can do this straight away. Adults often need time to process an event before they apologise. It is fine to allow them some time before they try to mend the relationship. You can say, "It's okay if you don't feel ready to apologise yet. It can be hard to do this straight away. Take some time. I'm here if you need some help."

Having your child recognise the need to say sorry is a good start. But quite frankly, saying sorry may not be enough. Apologising is often like a band-aid or bandage. If we cut ourselves, a dressing will help it heal quicker, but it isn't instant. Kids sometimes expect the other person to get over what happened quickly since they said sorry. The band-aid analogy can help them understand that "Sorry" doesn't fix everything.

Talk to your child about how the relationship has changed since the event and how they need to try to improve it. Saying sorry is a good start, but help them to understand that they may need to do more. Have them think about what else they could do, then have them try it. They can ask the other person, "Does that help?" This is the beginning for both children to learn about conflict resolution. It doesn't mean the offending child has to do whatever the other child wants, but it does help them realise that when we damage a relationship, it can take time to mend.

Modelling

The best way to teach children empathy and how to mend relationships is to model it. As parents, we are going to make mistakes. That is guaranteed.

Working to repair our relationship with our children when we make mistakes is one of the best ways to teach them how to do this for themselves. It can be hard as parents to own up to mistakes without sharing the blame. It can be very tempting to say, "I'm sorry, but you shouldn't..." If we model taking ownership of our behaviour, our kids will see how it is done and learn what forgiving is like.

When we get caught up in the controversy about saying the words, "I'm sorry," we miss the point. We really want our children to become empathetic and understand that when we hurt others, we need to mend the relationship. This lesson is far more important than mindlessly insisting kids say, "I'm sorry."

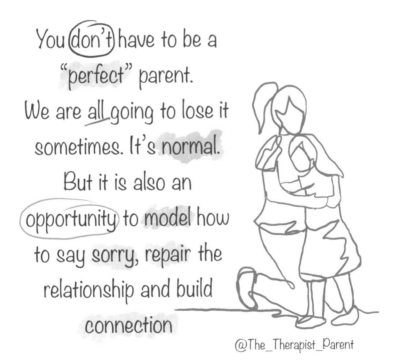

You don't have to be a "perfect" parent. We are all going to lose it sometimes. It's normal. But it is also an opportunity to model how to say sorry, repair the relationship and build connection

@The_Therapist_Parent

Emotion Coaching Cheat Sheet

Emotion coaching is the basis of helping children recognise feelings in themselves and others, self-regulation, empathy, and problem-solving. That's why it is an vital step in helping children mend relationships.

While emotion coaching is an incredible tool to have in your parenting toolbox, there are times that you shouldn't use it (Gottman, 1997).

When Not to Emotion Coach

1.When you are in a hurry. It's not something that can be rushed and it really won't be effective.

2.In Public. Don't do it in front of their friends or anywhere that they may be embarrassed. If they are feeling self-conscious, they won't be able to see beyond their own feelings.

3.If they aren't safe. If they are about to run out on the road, you aren't going to stop and emotion coach before you grab them.

How to Emotion Coach

Recognise they are struggling.	"You seem upset." "Wow, this looks really hard." "Oh, I can tell something isn't working for you."
Be curious about the emotion.	"You seem really angry, is that right?" "That seems frustrating, is it?' "New things can be scary, can't they?"
Validate the emotion.	"I get frustrated when things don't go the way I want, too." "It is hard when things don't work." "Sometimes, I get nervous in new places, too."
Help them calm.	"Would you like a hug?" "How about we match our breathing." "I am here when you need me."
Problem-solve together.	"What could we do next time?" "How would you like things to be different?"

Next time an opportunity comes to emotion coach with your child, write down what you did and what the outcome was.

Is Praise Bad?

There is a lot of talk in parenting circles about praise and whether we should be praising our kids. For a generation or so, parents were told to give their kids lots of praise, to catch them being 'good.' We have heard repeatedly that we should tell our kids they are doing a 'good job,' that they are a 'good girl/boy,' or other general and positive feedback. Now, we are being told that we shouldn't be doing it at all; that praise can actually be harmful. So, is praise bad?

Research has shown that not all praise is good (Henderlong and Lepper, 2002). There are aspects of praise that can actually be damaging. However, this doesn't mean that we stop speaking positively to our kids. They still need encouragement. We just need to be specific with how we give praise.

Why Some Praise Doesn't Work

If we say general things to our kids, such as, "You're so smart" or, "You're so clever," we do not recognise the effort needed to achieve. Research has shown that children who receive praise for intelligence are actually less likely to succeed (Mueller and Dweck, 1998). Children who believe they are 'smart' often also think they should do well without effort. There is no intrinsic motivation to try, as they feel this should occur without them having to work at it. Another study has also found that children who are told that they are 'smart' are less likely to take risks in fear that they may 'fail.' The belief is that if they fail, they will no longer be 'smart,' 'clever,' or whatever they have been told (Brummelman et al, 2014). When we use these general labels, we also send the message that people are either 'smart/talented' or not. Such classification leaves no room for improvement or getting better if you believe it is something you don't have control over. Ultimately, in this circumstance, children will feel helpless to change.

Praise can also seem conditional and controlling. If we generally say, "Good girl/boy," does this mean when we don't praise the child, they are 'bad?' It leaves a child feeling as though their acceptance is dependent on their behaviour and not on them as a person.

When praise is used as a way to control behaviour, the chances are kids will push against it.

Manipulation gets resistance, even if it is through praise. By around the age of five years, children can tell when your praise is sincere and when it is just a way to get them to do what you want them to do (Mizokawa, 2018).

So, if praise is just a blanket label (good boy/girl) or is focused on a child's ability alone (you are so smart), then it often won't work, and it might just have the opposite outcome than we had hoped. It also has the potential to damage our relationship with our children as they feel that their acceptance is conditional on our praise.

So, What Should We Do?

Focus on Effort

When we praise our kids, we need to ensure we recognise the effort it took to achieve, not just the achievement itself. You can say, "I noticed you tried to sound out those words and didn't give up" or, "Wow, you worked hard on that." Rather than, "You are such a good reader." When we focus on the effort involved, our children feel like they have made progress. Directing attention in this way builds their self-esteem because the effort they put in results in the desired outcome. It also means they see that progress comes from effort. As does the motivation to do things for themselves.

Be Honest

We aren't doing our kids any favours by telling them we think they were the best runner, even though they lost the race. It is okay to tell the truth if it is done constructively. The child might not have done well because they are younger and smaller than the others in the class. You might also know that the child who won practises their technique and runs every day. Maybe your child didn't practise at all and has no interest in running. If we honestly point out why they may not have done well, that can give them the opportunity to improve. But again, be careful of blanket labels. Don't say, "You just aren't a runner" or, "I can't run either." That doesn't leave room for improvement or the need to focus on the effort they put in.

Show Gratitude

When we say thank you to our children, they feel appreciated. When we feel appreciated and valued, we feel better about ourselves.

All of us, whether a child or an adult, will do more of something that makes us feel appreciated. Instead of saying, "Good job cleaning your room," you could say, "Thank you for cleaning your room. I really appreciate it." When we do this, kids also see how what they do impacts others and that the impact can be positive for everyone.

Give Attention

The biggest motivator for our kids is our time and connection with them. A child will feel more confident in their abilities if we spend time engaged with them in what they are doing rather than just giving throw-away praise and general comments. If we sit with a child while they draw a picture and talk to them about the colours they use or what the picture is about, they will gain much more than they would from a, "Good drawing" comment. When we give our support and show interest in what they are doing, there is no need to praise the outcome; they are already receiving what they need from doing the task and having you connect with them.

So, Is Praise Bad?

Some forms of praise can definitely be harmful or at least counterproductive. As I have mentioned, when we give general statements of praise or focus on ability, we can actually reduce motivation, negatively impact self-esteem, and even cause our kids to rebel against what we are trying to encourage. However, when we focus on the effort, be honest with them, show gratitude, and foster connection with our children, they are more likely to build their self-esteem and, ultimately, be more motivated.

If we want children to have intrinsic motivation and not rely on rewards....

- Ask if they feel proud of themselves

- Praise them for the effort

- Talk about how good it feels when you finish something

@The_Therapist_Parent

110

Praise Alternatives

None of us mean any harm when we say, "Good job." We are usually just busy and want to offer some praise. It can become a habit though and sound insincere. It can take a bit of time to break this habit, and sometimes it's hard to think of what else to say or do.

Here are some ideas:

Don't Say Anything: Our attention can be the best form of praise. Sometimes, just a smile, a hug, or a thumbs up is enough encouragement. Spending time with your child while they read is going to have a far greater impact than yelling out, "Good reading" from across the kitchen.

Say Thank You: When we say thank you to our children, they feel appreciated. Instead of saying, "Good job picking up your toys," you could say, "Thank you for picking up your toys. I really appreciate it." When we do this, kids also see how what they do impacts others and that the impact can be positive for everyone.

Be specific: When we praise our kids, we need to ensure that we recognise the effort it took to achieve, not just the achievement itself. You can say, "That was really hard and you didn't give up" or, "Wow, you worked hard on that." When we focus on the effort involved, our children feel like they have made progress. Directing attention in this way builds their self-esteem because the effort they put in results in the desired outcome.

III

Good thinking. You worked hard on that.

I love the colours you used.

You have improved so much. You are right.

Now you've figured it out! You're really improving.

I knew you could do it.

Keep working on it; you're improving. You must have been practicing.

You did a lot of work today. You are learning fast.

Couldn't have done it better myself.

That's an interesting way of looking at it.

You're getting better and better.

That's a good point.

I knew you could do it. You put a lot of detail into your picture.

It looks like you've put a lot of work into this.

Your studying really paid off. That shows dedication.

You coloured the sky blue and the house purple (describe what you see).

That took a lot of imagination.

That was a brave decision. Hugs. Thank you.

You really demonstrated good sportsmanship tonight.

How creative.

You guys worked together to repair the fort, great teamwork!

You remembered.

What a responsible choice. That shows a lot of courage.

Can you tell me more about your drawing?

Which part do you like the best?

Can you show me how you built this Lego tower?

Thank you for being so patient.

That was very thoughtful. That took a lot of patience.

4.

Common Struggles

Why Is My Child Lying?

Most parents are horrified when their child lies. But the truth is, it's normal. Lying is a sign of a significant developmental stage. It tends to start at about two–five years of age, when 'theory of mind' begins to develop. 'Theory of mind' is a critical stage of development when a child becomes aware that other people have thoughts, feelings, and beliefs that are different from theirs. It is the foundation of some essential social skills, and we literally can't have empathy without it. But it also gives us the ability to lie. Studies have even reported that lying in young children is a sign of intelligence (Alloway et al, 2015). However, that doesn't mean that we celebrate when our kids lie. We still want to encourage honesty, but it probably isn't something to be overly concerned about.

Why Do Kids Lie?

To Avoid Punishment

Kids most commonly lie because they don't want to get into trouble. Nobody likes to suffer the consequences when they know they have done something wrong. It makes sense that a child would lie to try to avoid this. Really, it shouldn't be surprising that kids don't want to tell their parents something they think they will get into trouble for. Parents often push kids into a corner, baiting them by asking if they have done something when we know they have. For example, "Did you eat the chocolate?" When they have chocolate all over their face. We think we are giving them an opportunity to tell the truth, but really, we are putting them on the spot, and they react out of fear. There are better ways to get the truth. Instead, we should just say, "I see you have eaten the chocolate." You can then ask them to consider how they think that would make you feel and why you might be disappointed by what they did.

Punishing a child for lying is not going to stop the lying. It will just make them try harder to be better at it, to avoid punishment. We need to coach our kids to understand when lies are most harmful, how they affect others, and even how they feel when they lie. By doing this, we allow our kids to understand why lying is an inappropriate choice rather than something that gets you punished.

We also need to focus on when children are honest, and emphasise that this is a positive. Even if they tell you they did something wrong, thank them for being honest. Then work through what has happened together, getting them involved in fixing the problem.

To Compensate for Low Self-Esteem

Have you ever heard kids say they scored all the points in a game? Or, how they did amazing things you knew couldn't be true? People often think that these children are egotistical and 'need to be brought down a peg or two.' When in fact the opposite is true. When kids tell grandiose lies that make them look good, it is usually because they don't believe they measure up. They embellish reality to seek approval. These kids don't need to be brought down; they need to be lifted up. It is essential they feel good about themselves and recognise their strengths.

We definitely shouldn't punish our kids or make them feel bad if they lie like this. That will only make them feel worse. However, it is not wise to ignore this behaviour completely. When you know your child has made up a lie to try to make themselves look good, have a conversation about it. Explain, "I know that it didn't happen like that. You don't have to try to impress me. I already love so much about you." You could ask them why they said what they did. But they may not really know. Often, they just wished it happened that way. Direct your focus toward what your child is good at and the characteristics you love about them. Activities such as the *Self-Esteem Bucket* (on page 233) and the *Tree of Me* (on page 236) can benefit children in this situation.

To Test What Would Happen

Avoiding punishment isn't the only reason kids lie. Sometimes, kids lie because they want to see what will happen. They are testing people's reactions and determining the consequences. It can be a way to test the waters before they actually go ahead with something. This could be a positive or negative thing; possibly something they don't yet have the confidence to do. They could also be practising lying to see when it does and doesn't work.

Parents might cringe at the idea of their kids practising lying, but if you think about it, adults lie a lot. They have a better idea of when it is okay and when it isn't.

Telling a friend you have an appointment when they ask you to go out because you really just want to stay home is a socially acceptable lie. We barely think anything of it because we know we did it to spare our friend's feelings. But kids are still learning this 'skill.' And it is a 'skill' that, like everything else we learn as children, takes time to master and develop.

Some lies that don't cause harm or compensate for low self-esteem can probably be ignored. Remember, it is normal; we don't need to make a big deal of every lie. However, you could say, "I'm not sure about that," or something similar, so the child knows you are aware it isn't the truth. But there is no need to overreact.

They Speak before They Think

Some kids, particularly those who are impulsive, may speak before they have thought through what has happened. It may seem like they are lying because they change their story, but may have just answered before they recalled all the information. When this happens, we need to make sure we give them enough time to process everything. Don't feel as though this is just giving them time to make up a story. It simply provides the opportunity to put their memories in order.

Sometimes, kids actually believe what they have said. Especially if they have spoken impulsively, forgotten there was more to the story or done more than they should have. For example, they might think they have put their clothes away, but they got distracted halfway through and didn't finish the task. If this occurs, providing visual checklists, timers, or other ways to stay on task and be more organised can be handy.

There are many reasons why kids lie. It could be to avoid punishment, to improve their self-image, to test boundaries, or simply because they are impulsive. Whatever the reason, we need to remember that lying is normal and is an integral part of personal and social development. Punishing kids for lying will generally make them try to improve their lies and lower their self-esteem. Instead, we need to look at the reason for the lie and help them grow from there.

When our child lies

@The_Therapist_Parent

we can worry

We did something wrong

I have to stop it quickly

How will they turn out?

But

It is a normal part of development

Sibling Rivalry and What to Do about It

All parents want their kids to get along. Wouldn't it be wonderful if everyone was always happy and our kids loved playing together without any conflict? But the reality is that we have kids who scream, "Mum, he's looking out MY window!" "Stop looking at me!" and "He is breathing loudly to annoy me."

The truth is, we can't expect kids to get along all the time just because they are related. Adults don't get along all the time, and we have a choice about who we spend time and share our lives with. Kids often have to share a room, toys, the bathroom, and their parent's time. And they have no say in it. When we think of it like that, it is no wonder there is sibling rivalry.

So, is sibling rivalry just something we should expect and put up with? It may be inevitable, but it isn't all bad. What better place to learn to negotiate and manage conflict than in a family that is always there to practise with. It is much better for kids to learn how to deal with conflict in the home than in the playground or, worse, as adults. If we see sibling rivalry as an opportunity to learn skills that will help them in the future, then it seems far less scary. Having said that, we don't want to just leave our kids to 'fight it out.' That's definitely not a skill you want them to carry into adulthood. If we can guide them through constructively managing the conflict rather than simply shutting it down, they will learn essential life skills.

Causes of Sibling Rivalry

Jealousy: One of the main causes of sibling rivalry arises because children want their parent's attention, and another child seems to be getting more of it. This is a fact that can feel exhausting for parents. Who has time to give a demanding child more attention? As parents, we can feel that our kids already take up all of our time. We can't imagine how they could possibly want more. If you consider the cause of the fights, there is usually some evidence of jealousy. Fighting over who sits next to you, who does something first, or constantly finding fault so the other child 'gets into trouble' are all signs of jealousy. Such behaviour stems from wanting to be seen as better than the other child.

The good news is that helping our kids feel connected to us and get the attention they need doesn't have to take a long time. But it does require focused attention. Even just 10–15 minutes of one-on-one time with a child, doing something they have chosen, can be enough for them to feel as though their needs have been met. Providing this attention means children don't feel they have to fight for it.

Ideally, you would spend some time engaged with each child every day. While this isn't always practical, especially in large families, there are ways you can work around it. One idea is to allow each child to stay up a little later one night a week to have some special time with their parent. It can also help to label this time as special and hold boundaries around it so other children realise its importance. For example, "It's Mum and [number two child's] time right now. I will help you with your homework once we are finished." By doing this, the child knows that this time was especially for them and not incidental, and other children know they will receive the same treatment.

A critical factor of sibling rivalry is that you recognise when your child is acting out of jealousy and not just being difficult. Rather than punishing the child and sending them away (which will only make the behaviour worse), try to set aside some one-on-one time to see if their behaviour improves.

Boredom: Sometimes sibling fighting is a matter of boredom, and the rivalry is simply to increase stimulation. Have you ever noticed on a long drive, one child keeps touching or staring at the other as if they will do anything just to get a reaction? Or, on the weekend, when everyone is home, one kid just has to keep annoying the other? Obviously, this behaviour isn't acceptable, but it can help to see the cause so we can do something about it.

The best strategy to reduce rivalry due to boredom is to prepare in advance. For long car trips, have your kids choose activities they want to do. While I wouldn't normally advocate it, screens are beneficial at these times. When restricted in a car or travelling by other means, devices can provide a wealth of education and entertainment. Although, I encourage you to have other options as well. If kids are fighting at home due to boredom, you can step in with activities they can do separately. Or alternatively, provide something the whole family can do together.

Conflict: Sometimes, rivalry arises out of everyday friction. Nobody gets on all the time. We all have conflicts, and that's okay. But it is important to deal with it productively. Conflict contrasts with our desires and can help us see where things need to change. It also provides an opportunity for us to express our needs. But it does take practise.

We must not jump in too soon when guiding kids' conflict management. Hang back and see if they can work things out on their own. If the situation escalates or gets physical, then you will have to step in. But for the most part, we want kids to practise resolving these situations for themselves, not relying on you to umpire all the time.

If you must step in, allow everyone to calm down enough before you have them consider the situation. Children may need a little time on their own before they can do this effectively. You can then follow the steps below to help your children better understand the situation.

Identify the Problem: Identifying the problem is the start of any successful conflict resolution, whether you are a child or an adult. Young children will likely need you to define the problem for them. For example, "It looks like you both want that swing." From there, try to get them to understand how the other person feels. Then have each explain what is upsetting them. If they are too young or can't express their feelings, label it for them. "So, you are frustrated that they got on the swing before you." When they know what the problem really is, and how everyone feels, they will have a better chance at brainstorming an acceptable solution.

Problem Solving: One great strategy that works with kids aged three and older is to give them five minutes to conduct their own 'meeting' to figure out a plan to solve the problem. Kids respond well to being given responsibility and independence. However, explain that you will be close by if they need you to help. After they have had a 'meeting,' they must present their solution to you. If it's acceptable, they can continue playing to test if it worked. The idea behind this strategy is that they must work together to come to a mutually acceptable conclusion. If their solution seems unfair, or you don't think it will work, then talk them through it. Get children to consider each other in relation to their idea, e.g.,

"If you do that, how will your brother feel?" or, "Will you feel happy if your sister has more time with the toy than you do?" Such questions move the focus from what is suitable for one person to what is fair for everyone.

Plan Ahead: It is always a good idea to practise conflict resolution before friction begins. If your children often fight in a particular game, go through some ideas they can implement before they start playing. Explore all the 'what if's' they can think of. For example, "What will you do if you both want the same Lego pieces?" Help them devise a plan first and allow them to see that if they can't resolve any conflict, they won't have fun playing the game. In these instances, you don't have to threaten punishment. Just make them aware that unresolved conflict will bring their game to an end.

Sibling rivalry and conflict are not bad. It is the practise ground for recognising feelings and, with the help of their parents, helps them meet their needs. Remember, as parents, we must recognise what triggers our children and guide them through conflict resolution so they develop the skills necessary for a lifetime of social interaction.

Young children can't understand sharing. It is a developmental milestone that they haven't reached. Forcing them won't make them develop quicker

@The_Therapist_Parent

Conflict Resolution Activities

The best way to manage conflict is to be proactive. Conflict is going to happen at some point with our children. If we can have them practise the skills ahead of time, it will be easier to do than trying to learn these skills while emotions are high. If we make it fun, children are more likely to be involved and learn.

Conflict Resolution Role-Play

I know parents tend to hate role-play games, but kids love them. They are such a good way for children to physically try out what they have learnt and put themselves in other people's shoes. Write down common conflicts that your children have and get them to act out each one. Then talk about possible solutions to how the problem could be solved. Then try it again. How does everyone feel? Did it work? Should they try something else?

Story Time - What Might Happen Next?

Read a story together, preferably one they don't know by heart, and as you read, stop and brainstorm what could happen next? This helps children realise that there are lots of different choices in every situation. Ask, "What do you think they are thinking?" or, "How do you think they would feel?" By doing this you are building their ability to see other's perspective and build empathy.

Draw It Out (Ages Seven and Up)

Get a blank sheet of paper and coloured pencils. Using either a real scenario or a made up one, have children describe what happened, from start to finish, from one point of view. Then, choose another colour and brainstorm three possible solutions to the problem that might work. Next, ask them to think about the other's perspective and try to retell the story. This can be difficult and might take a few tries. Ask them to pick another colour to represent the other perspective and brainstorm three possible solutions that might work for the other person. Finally, ask your child to look for the common ground. Is there a solution that might work for both? If not, brainstorm three more solutions that meet in the middle. By looking at the struggle from different perspectives, children learn to empathise with others and look for solutions that help everyone involved.

Raising Appreciative Kids

Most parents hope their kids appreciate what they have. Many also wish their kids would express their gratitude occasionally. Parents who are busy juggling life and constantly take their children to activities then hear their children whining, "Why can't I have a [name current desire]. Other kids are allowed one." Or, "I want a [name new desire]." It feels as though our kids don't appreciate everything they already have. As a parent, it can be extremely infuriating to hear your kids be ungrateful. But gratitude is not something that comes naturally. It has to be taught and practised.

Often, our expectations of appreciation and gratitude are just too high for our children's developmental levels. Yes, we can start teaching gratitude early, but children can't fully understand other people's perspectives until at least five–seven years of age. They are absolutely the centre of their own universe and believe they are the centre of everyone else's too.

To feel and express gratitude and appreciation, you need to be able to understand another's perspective. It means that you can comprehend the effort someone has put in or how others are different from you. This is not a skill that young children have. Luckily, it is something that will develop and grow when taught.

How Do We Build Gratitude and Appreciation

Saying "No"

There is more to appreciation and gratitude than just saying "No," but it is still significant. Often, parents don't realise how much they give their kids. I got into the habit of buying my kids a small chocolate every time I had to put fuel in the car. I like doing nice things for my kids, the chocolates were cheap, and I rarely noticed how much they were when buying fuel. However, what my actions did was set up an expectation. I soon started to resent the kids' wanting a chocolate every time I got fuel. But it really wasn't their fault. I had set up that expectation.

This type of passive consumerism is widespread. It is the small toy bought every time you go to the shops or the chocolate milk from the supermarket. There is certainly no judgement on your parenting here.

Sometimes, doing this to get through a full grocery shop with your sanity intact is self-care, especially when your children are young. However, we need to be careful about the expectations we create for our children. We can't really get upset with them for wanting something everywhere we go when we have always bought them something everywhere we go!

When we do start to say "No" to our kids, it will to feel to them like we are the most unfair parent in the world. Try not to get too upset by this. It is not personal. Your children are not considering the money you have spent all the other times you have bought them something and how many things they already have. All they can see is that they didn't get what they usually get. Wait until they have moved through the emotion, and then tell them you understand that the situation is disappointing. Let them know you 'get it.' Usually, you would buy them something. Then explain why you only do that sometimes. You can remind them of the many things they do have, just not in a way that shames them. Saying, "You have so many things, and you don't appreciate them," is not going to help. You could, however, say, "Can you think of fun things that we do together?" Or, "What are your favourite toys?" This shifts the focus from what they want and can't have, to what they do already have and enjoy. This is the building block of gratitude.

Say "Thank You"

I'm not suggesting you enforce a begrudging, "Thank you" from your child. Forcing a child to give thanks when they aren't thankful does not teach them appreciation. However, I think that children need to be taught that saying, "Thank you" is important because it helps the other person feel happy and appreciated. Rather than asking them to say thank you, you could explain that when we are given something or someone does something for us, we should say thank you so the other person feels good. They might still need a reminder sometimes, but if they understand why we do it, they are more likely to say it and mean it.

It is not only kids who need to express their thanks. Parents must model this if they want their children to do it too. Kids need to see you say, "Thank you" to the shop assistant, waitress, your partner, and especially to them. If we want our kids to be grateful, we need them to know what it feels like when someone is thankful for them. It is much easier for a child to understand why we express our thanks when they experience your thanks.

Let them feel the joy of being appreciated so that they can share this with others. Be specific when you say, "Thank you" so they know what you are grateful for and how it made you or others feel. For example, don't just say, "Thank you for sharing." Say, "Thank you for sharing with your sister. I can see how happy she is because you shared."

Give Responsibility

Too often, parents do everything for their children and then get upset because their kids don't appreciate what is done for them. How are children supposed to appreciate these things if they have never done them? How do they know how hard and time-consuming housework can be if someone else has always done it? This doesn't mean that your children need long lists of jobs. But as they get older, they can take on more responsibility. Just like learning to walk and feed themselves, children can eventually learn to dress themselves, pick up their toys, clean their room, and help with dinner. When we do too much for our children, we rob them of opportunities to practise independence and build a sense of achievement and self-esteem.

A part of teaching kids to appreciate what is done for them is having them help you do what needs to be done. Some parents might cringe at this, as tasks are often easier without 'help.' But when children do simple chores with you, like cutting vegetables, or passing you the washing to put on the clothesline, they get to experience the effort you put in. Make sure to take advantage of the positive conversations and fun you can have doing this together, too.

Money Management

There is much controversy around whether we should pay kids pocket money. And if so, whether it should be paid for doing chores or given without expectation. There are better places for such a discussion, but it is important to teach children how to manage money and save for things they want.

Laura Higgins, Senior Executive Leader – Financial Capability at the Australian Securities and Investments Commission (ASIC), has many ideas on teaching our children about money. It is suggested that from a young age, children can have three jars labelled Saving, Spending, and Giving. When your child is given money, they divide it into the three jars.

Depending on your child's maturity, you can decide how much goes into each category, or you can negotiate this. This allows the child to see the money and watch it grow. But they also learn that not all money is for personal spending. The Giving jar is especially relevant as it helps children understand that there are people who need help and that they can contribute.

Practice Giving

It is crucial for a child's social development that they realise there is more than just their little family. They need to see that some people have more and some have less, but we can help one another by contributing. Having parents model this behaviour allows children to see this value in action and experience the difference it makes to all involved. You might sponsor a child your children can help write letters to, you could choose gifts for a toy drive, or take a meal to someone when they are sick. If children see that some people have less than they do, or need help, they will find it harder to feel entitled.

We can't expect our children to automatically show appreciation and gratitude. It is not something that just happens. Developmentally, it can take a while for children to see beyond themselves. It is up to us to teach our kids to be grateful. We have to set boundaries, show them what it is like to experience being appreciated, give them responsibility, and show them the importance of giving. Then our kids can learn to be appreciative. We just need to show them how.

If we want our children to be grateful, empathetic and show appreciation, then <u>we</u> need to gratitude , empathy and appreciation towards <u>them</u>

@The_Therapist_Parent'

Teaching Gratitude

We all know that we should be grateful. We know that it helps us feel good and appreciate what we have. But practising gratitude regularly impacts much more than just how we feel. Robert Emmon (2004) has over 20 years of research into gratitude and found some amazing results. The studies found that people who regularly practise gratitude experience physical, psychological, and social benefits. Significantly, when children learn to be grateful, they are less likely to develop anxiety and depression in adulthood.

Gratitude, like everything, needs to be learned. While some personality types will be more likely to see the positive aspects of their lives, everyone needs to become aware of what they have. Being grateful is something we all need to practise, but it can be particularly difficult for young children. Children under the age of six have not developed the ability to see things from another's perspective or a 'theory of mind,' so we need to make sure our expectations of them aren't too high.

We can't expect young children to appreciate what others have done for them, as they don't understand that the actions were generous. That doesn't mean that we shouldn't start teaching gratitude. It just means we shouldn't expect children to say, "Thank you so much for getting up and making my breakfast. I know you would rather stay in bed." But they can learn to appreciate the taste of their toast or the warmth of a hug. The benefits of gratitude are overwhelming for people of all ages.

The Benefits of Gratitude

(Sourced from research by Emmon, 2004.)

Physical:

- The **immune system** has been shown to improve with engagement in gratitude. Hopefully, this means there will be fewer snotty noses and sick days.
- **Lowered stress and blood pressure.** The body's ability to cope with stressful situations improves with a regular gratitude practice.
- **Improved sleep**. When we feel happier, we relax, our brain calms, and we are more likely to drift off to sleep easily. For children, this can mean not waking up as often during the night.

Psychological:

- Feeling **happier and more optimistic**. When we look for the good in our lives, our mood improves. When our mood is improved there are definite ripple effects for all those around us. Let's face it, life feels better for you and everyone around you when you feel happier.
- Increased **alertness and awareness**. An integral part of being grateful involves actively looking for the good around you. In doing this, you raise your awareness, both generally and of positive events you may have otherwise missed. This adjustment in our attention means we are less likely to 'switch off' and more likely to **focus** on what is necessary.
- **Increased self-esteem** is another benefit. When we prime ourselves to look for the good around us, we also see the good within us. We notice the love and support we have, and we recognise that we are valued and worthy.
- Improved **resilience**. Being grateful doesn't mean that everything works out all the time. It means we can see positive aspects in situations and ways to improve, even when things don't go as we had hoped. Therefore, we cope better when things go wrong and are willing to try again.
- **Decreased Anxiety and Depression**. We know that thoughts, feelings, and behaviours are connected. When we improve our way of thinking, we improve our mood. In the long term, this helps prevent anxiety and depression.

Social

- Tendency to become more helpful, **generous, empathetic, and compassionate**. When we see the good in life and the positive things people do for us, we are more likely to feel compelled to help in return. Remember, this is difficult for children under the age of six, but if we assist them with seeing what they can be grateful for, this trait will develop more easily.
- We are more likely to **forgive** others when we realise that we all make mistakes and need help from time to time.
- Improvements in **friendships and relationships**. Gratitude generally results in feeling happier and appreciating what others do for us. As everyone likes to feel appreciated, improvements in our relationships often result.

129

- Often, people become more outgoing as they are not as concerned with making mistakes or suffering negative consequences; they are more willing to try new things.

<u>So, Exactly What is Gratitude?</u>

Gratitude involves being able to recognise and appreciate all that is around and within you. When you look for the positives, you magnify the pleasure you get from life as you realise just how much good there is. Gratitude also relies on focusing on what you have rather than what you lack. It is a skill that needs to be taught and modelled, it doesn't come naturally. It is unrealistic to expect kids (or adults) to automatically be grateful for all that they have. There are some ideas for activities you can do with your child, in the next section, which can help them develop this trait.

Gratitude benefits us physically, psychologically, and socially. But we need to teach, practise, and develop this skill. If children can be taught to develop this when they are young, they will cultivate a thinking style that ultimately improves their enjoyment and success throughout life.

Practicing gratitude does so much more than you think

@The_Therapist_Parent

Improves mood

Increases alertness

Improved self esteem

Resilience

Less anxiety and depression

Learning Gratitude Activities

Gratitude involves learning to focus on what you have and seeing the good in it. This is something that isn't easy and takes practice. The more we practise gratitude with our children, the easier it will become for them to express throughout their life. Here are some fun activities you can do with your child to help develop this skill.

Give Thanks: Make gratitude a part of your routine. Each night at the dinner table or before bed, make time for everyone to share what they were grateful for about their day. Children need to see that even though it may have felt like a 'bad' day, there are always things to be grateful for. When you do this as a family, children gain an understanding of what others appreciate too. Encourage children to get creative during this activity. Especially if this has been a part of your routine for some time, it is easy to fall into the trap of repeating some of the more obvious things you are grateful for.

While saying, "I am grateful for my house/family/food" may be true, you will begin to lose your depth of appreciation if this is your standby response. Encourage everyone to consider specific ways their lives have improved. What have they learned that they didn't know or couldn't do before? Did they see something beautiful that day? What things made them smile? (I have created 'gratitude cards' to help with this activity. These can be found on my website.)

Keep a Record: Another way you can celebrate gratefulness together is to have a Gratitude Jar. Whenever someone in your family feels grateful, they write their reason on a slip of paper and put it in a jar. At the end of the week or month, sit down together and read out everything everyone was grateful for. This is a great way to express appreciation for each other while building gratitude.

Older children can also be encouraged to keep a Gratitude Journal. When we write down what we are grateful for, it seems to make it more real. It also becomes a reference to look at when things aren't going well.

You can review your journal when you need a reminder of the positives in your life. This is especially relevant if you are feeling down and need a reminder of how quickly and unexpectedly your feelings can change for the better.

Expressing Thanks: Thanking people makes us feel happier, and the people around us feel appreciated. Make saying thank you to others a regular practice. Have your kids draw a picture to thank Grandma for the clothes they bought or give their teacher a letter showing that they appreciate what they do. Let your kids see you saying thank you to those around you as well: thank the shop assistant for taking the time to help; thank your neighbour for bringing your bin in from the street. But most importantly, say thank you to your kids. When they feel appreciated, they will learn what that is like and be more likely to appreciate others.

Helping Others: When we help others, we begin to appreciate what we have and how fortunate we are. We are less likely to be self-centred, and we gain access to a bigger picture. Children will need help developing these skills; visual reminders are a good resource.

For example, you could have your children choose a charity they want to support. Keep a jar on the bench that you can all contribute money to. You might put spare change in it, do fundraising, or have them donate part of their pocket money. When the jar is full, the money can be given to their chosen cause. Such a commitment is a regular reminder to focus on gratitude. Other ideas you could try are donating food or toys to charity or carrying out random acts of kindness. This leads to positive feelings and greater connections with others, again encouraging gratitude.

Helping around the house can build gratitude too. It provides an opportunity for children to understand the importance of working together and helps them appreciate what others do for them, too.

Mindfulness: Focusing on the present and what is around you is integral to mindfulness and gratitude. You can do this by going for a mindful walk, where you pay attention to what you see, feel, hear, and smell. You will find more mindfulness activities in the article *Mindfulness for Children* on page 188.

What to Do When You Have a Negative Thinker

Children are all very different. It is incredible to see that kids in the same family, with similar genetics and upbringing, can be complete opposites. Each child has their own temperament, which is thought to occur right from birth. Some children are outgoing, bubbly, and optimistic. Others are shy, reserved, and have a pessimistic view of things. Then, there are combinations of these.

As a psychologist who quite literally makes a living from helping children challenge negative thoughts and develop a growth mindset, I find it difficult when my son sees the world in a pessimistic light. We could have had a fantastic day, but he will find the one thing that went wrong and fixate on that. My other children aren't like that at all. They can find the positive in most situations. It has taken me some time to come to terms with the fact that this is his temperament and that it isn't all bad.

There are positives and negatives for all temperaments, and many different personality types. But one thing we all agree on is that everyone has unique strengths and difficulties. Children like my son, who can be a 'glass half empty' thinker, can also be very cautious and analytical. He likes things to be 'just right,' to have all the details worked out, and he can be quite serious. Other kids, who might be really outgoing and bubbly, might not consider the consequences of situations and act more impulsively. Whatever their temperament, our kids need to know that they are fine just as they are. But we can still work on the limitations.

We know that a negative thinking style is linked to depression in adults, so while we don't want to change our kid's personalities, we do want to support them to think in a more balanced way. Kids like my son won't be the ones to see the light in every situation or go bouncing from one happy feeling to another. Still, they can learn not to get stuck in a sea of negatives.

When examining how children think, we look toward their 'attribution style.' Someone's style, or outlook, generally falls more toward optimism or pessimism. It can be helpful to explain this using a specific example. Let's say your child performs poorly in a spelling test at school. The pessimistic attribution style will think that the challenge is **Internal, Pervasive, and Permanent.**

133

So, in this situation, they would think, "I am hopeless at spelling" (Internal), "I can't do any schoolwork" (pervasive), and "I'm stupid" (permanent).

On the other hand, the optimistic attribution style, tends to be **External, Specific, and Temporary.** In this example, the child may think, "That was a really hard spelling test" (external), "I'm disappointed I got those words wrong" (specific), and "If I practise, I will do better next time" (temporary). Looking at our kid's thinking this way allows us to see that we don't have to change a cautious and analytical personality style. We can simply encourage more resilient thinking.

Don't be fooled, though. The optimistic attribution style is not all sunshine and rainbows. It looks at difficult situations realistically, acknowledging that some difficulties and challenges can make us feel bad. However, people with this attribution style are less likely to get stuck in their thoughts and fall into downward spirals.

Supporting our kids, regardless of their outlook, involves encouraging thoughts that are **External, Specific, and Temporary.**

The following are some examples of how we can assist this type of thinking:

You made a mistake this time. You will learn from it. **(External)**

You got two words wrong, but you got eight right. **(Specific)**

You can't do it yet. You will get it with practise. **(Temporary)**

What Else Can We Do to Help a Negative Thinker?

Show Empathy

We all have bad days and times of negative thinking. Kids are just like adults in this regard. They can be in a grumpy mood and feel like everything is going badly. It helps if our kids know that we understand their situation. Children don't really start to understand others' perspectives until about age five. So, when they feel like everything is bad, they can feel very alone. It can be helpful to share your experiences of 'bad' days you have had. Normalising difficult moods and challenges can help kids see that these things are not permanent. If we don't focus on our kid's feelings first, they will not be motivated to change their thinking style. If they don't think you understand their reasoning and why they feel that way, how would you know your way of thinking is better?

But if you say, "I know it feels like you can't do it, and that is very disappointing," they realise you understand their perspective. Give them time to grasp that you appreciate their position. Then, once they know you are on board, you can discuss their thoughts and add some positivity; for example, "It took you a while to learn to ride your bike, but now you are great at it."

Model Optimism

Our kids soak up everything we do and say. We may as well use this to our advantage. Let your kids see you frustrated or disappointed, but be sure to bring in optimistic thinking that is external, specific, and temporary. Speak out loud when things don't go according to plan, and model how to manage your thoughts to impact your mood. After you have been doing this for a while, it is amazing how your kids will start doing it too. I know I have said in frustration, "You always leave your towel on the floor!" the response was, "Not ALWAYS. I did tonight." As frustrating as that reply might be at the time, it is good to know our children can learn to manage their thoughts and share their approach with us.

Practise Gratitude

One of the most powerful ways to change perspective and attitude is to be grateful. But this isn't something we all do naturally, and it needs to be practised. Regularly ask your kids what they are thankful for. You could do it at the dinner table or at bedtime. It is particularly helpful to have a regular gratitude ritual. Get your kids to be as creative as possible when remembering what they are grateful for. Is it that they can walk? That they have friends? That they live in a house? It could be anything, as long as they genuinely feel thankful for it. A fun activity is to write down things we are grateful for that happen throughout the year and put them in a jar. Then, on New Year's Eve, open the jar and read each one aloud. It is a great way to look for the positives in your day and then reminisce about them together.

We know there are strengths and weaknesses in all temperament types. However, that doesn't mean kids with a more pessimistic thinking style shouldn't be encouraged to feel more positivity and optimism. We all have ways to learn and grow, and the way we think is no exception. Supporting all kids to have resilience in their thinking while celebrating who they are provides firm foundations for their future growth and enjoyment of life.

Always focusing on the positives can be hard, and not realistic.

You don't have to ignore the negatives

Try adding

What else is true?

@The_Therapist_Parent

Changing Mindset Activities

It is important for children to see that what we think, changes how we feel. When we can see mistakes and difficulties as a challenges rather than failures, their confidence, perseverance, and mood will improve. In order to help them, we need to be aware of our own self-talk and consciously direct them. Here are a few ways you can add these changes to your daily life.

Growth Mindset Questions to Ask

You can use these questions regularly to shift thinking to be more helpful:

- What did you do today that was hard? How did you work it out?
- What mistake did you make today? Did you learn from it?
- What would you like to get better at? How could you do that? What is something you have gotten better at recently?
- What's something you're curious about?
- What did you do today that made you think?
- What did you do today that you're proud of?

Affirmations to Repeat Regularly

- I try hard.
- I can do hard things.
- I keep trying, even when it's hard.
- Challenges make me stronger.
- If I can't do something, it's only because I haven't learned it or figured it out yet.
- I can learn new ways of doing things.
- Mistakes help me learn.

Make a Vision Board Together

Making vision boards is a fun activity that I do with my kids every New Year. A vision board will help them to look forward to the things they want to achieve. You can fill the vision board with photos/magazine cut outs of things they want to accomplish, things they hope to do more of, and inspiring quotes.

If you have a corkboard, have them pin the cutouts on it or stick them on cardboard and put them up in their room so they can see them every day.

Talk About Mistakes

Make talking about mistakes a normal part of life. Talk about your own mistakes and how you worked out how to fix things. As they do things and make mistakes, help them see the positives. Once they know what didn't work, what else could they do? This will help them point out what they've tried and what hasn't worked so they can make a plan for what might work.

Changing Unhelpful Thoughts Activity

When I talk to children about 'unhelpful' thoughts, or as Dr Tony Attwood (2014) calls them, "poisonous thoughts," I explain that these thoughts are any that make you feel 'not good.' They could make you feel sad, angry, frustrated, annoyed, etc. The premise behind this is that there is a relationship between thoughts, feelings, and behaviours. Our thoughts can trigger feelings, which then changes our behaviour.

Start by working out what their thoughts could be. You might need to work backwards from a situation. For example, "You punched your brother because he took your toy and wouldn't give it back." Then try to work out the the thought behind the behaviour, "You might think, that he always takes your stuff, and it's not fair." Write down as many thoughts as you can.

These thoughts usually have some common words. Such as Always, Never, Not Fair, Will. These extreme words can evoke intense emotions. Circle these words in their thoughts. I usually explain to kids that these unhelpful or poisonous thoughts have some truth to them but they aren't completely true, as these thoughts are exaggerated. We can then find the more helpful thought or 'antidote' thought.

The helpful thought or 'antidote' thought is not just the opposite of the unhelpful thought. If the unhelpful thought was, "He always take my stuff," the helpful thought wouldn't be, "He never takes my stuff," because that wouldn't be true either. A helpful thought is not supposed to make you feel wonderful, it is just supposed to help you feel a little bit better. When we can lift our mood a little it makes the situation easier to handle. So, for this example, the helpful thought could be, "He takes my stuff sometimes." Or, "He usually asks first." The child may still be a little upset, but not as much as they were with the extreme words. Work together to pick the best helpful thought or 'antidote.'

Often, after we have come up with the helpful thoughts, kids aren't convinced that this will help. What I do in this instance is get them to rate their mood out of 10 for the unhelpful thought, and then for the helpful thought. They are amazed to see the shift. Have your child write what their mood would be out of 10 (10 for feeling fantastic and 0 for feeling terrible) for each unhelpful thought. Then repeat the process for the helpful one. If there isn't a shift of at least three points, then you might need to find another helpful thought.

Learning to change our thoughts takes practise. It won't work instantly, but eventually, kids will start to recognise that they are using extreme words in their thinking and able to make adjustments. Be sure to talk about these thoughts when they are calm. Have them practise changing them when they are calm and, then, eventually, it will happen more automatically.

It Is Never Too Early to Prepare Kids for Social Media

We live in a world where social media is the norm. It is often the first place for communication – for just about everyone. Most schools and sporting organisations use social media as their main source of disseminating information. And the term 'Facebook friends' has become a well-understood way to describe a relationship.

This mechanism has become so ingrained in daily life. Yet, we usually don't start to educate our kids about it until just before they are legally old enough to use social media. The legal age for most social media apps is 13 years old, and while there is proactive education in most schools for children aged 11–12 years, some (Couglan, 2016) have shown that a massive three quarters of children aged 10–12 already use social media. The greatest concern is that we are beginning too late.

As a psychologist, I regularly work with children that are aged five–eight years old. You would think that social media is not really an issue for these kids. But if you ask them, they know what Facebook and Instagram are, and many of them have already made TikTok videos, with and without their parent's knowledge. When we truly understand the dangers of social media, it is terrifying to think how little education our kids have about it. We wouldn't let them cross the road without our guidance, yet some kids are thrown onto the 'busy highway' of social media and expected to keep themselves safe.

When I talk to parents about educating children about social media use, they seem to have one of two extreme responses. There is the strict, "My child won't be on social media" response and the, "They are fine, it's just social" response. Unfortunately, neither of these will help our kids manage the social media-driven world that we live in.

As much as we want to keep our kids safe from the dangers inherent in the design of social media, it is unrealistic to think that they won't be influenced by it, even if we manage to stop them from having an account. In some cases, keeping teenagers off social media altogether can actually cause harm. If most of their peers communicate this way, they could become isolated or ostracised by not having access.

Then again, giving free rein to a child or teenager with underdeveloped impulse control and problem-solving abilities could have devastating consequences.

One of the main reasons that navigating this aspect of parenting is so difficult is that we did not experience the world that our kids are growing up in; our adolescence was not overlaid with rapidly changing technology and instant communication. Sure, we may have experienced bullying, feeling left out, and many other common difficulties that come with growing up. But we weren't bombarded with a constant connection to the world at large. When we came home, most of us were removed from the pressures of the day. There was no cyber-bullying or concerns about how many 'likes' you received, and while there have always been issues with body image, we didn't have image filters and the ever-increasing pressure to look 'sexy.' So how do we educate our kids in a world we don't really understand? And when should we start?

Let's Start Young

I am definitely not advocating for young children to be on social media, However, it is not unusual to see toddlers using the internet to watch their favourite shows, play games, or make video calls. You may have set all the parental controls and be supervising, but that doesn't negate the need to explain the dangers.

Using a device can feel safe because it is in your home, but there are potential risks to letting things into your home, especially things you would not normally let in. Dr Kristy Goodwin (2021) says there are two main cyber-safety concerns facing parents of preschoolers; content and contact. The major cyber-safety content issues facing our preschoolers are their ready access to developmentally inappropriate content, such as scary or violent images and pornography. In addition, contact concerns include access to unknown people and paedophiles.

With children as young as three years old, you can lay the foundation for responsible and safe social media use by explaining that there are rules for using devices. It is important to impress that there are good and bad things on the internet and to stay safe. Just like there are rules for crossing the road, there are rules for using the internet.

Some good ground rules you could use include:

- **A parent or grown-up needs to be close.** No parental control will work better than your presence. Let children know they can't be in their room alone with a device; you need to be close enough to check on them. Really, this is no different from most parent's rules when taking kids to the park. To keep them safe, you need to see them and check that they are okay.

- **Tell someone if something comes up that makes you uncomfortable.** From an early age, kids need to learn that you are the person to go to if they see something they think is inappropriate. The last thing you want is for your child to be scared to tell you something for fear of 'getting in trouble.' Make it clear that you are there to help.

- **You can get lost on the internet.** As with the rest of life, don't press buttons if you don't know what they do. It is very easy to end up on sites that are not appropriate. Kids need to learn to stay safe on the sites you have approved.

- **Never talk to people you don't know.** Just as we would teach children not to go with strangers on the street, we need to explain that the same rules apply to the internet.

- **The need for privacy.** It is a good idea to explain the permanence of the Internet. Children aren't developmentally able to foresee the problems associated with sharing personal information, but you can start modelling the importance of keeping information private. Once data is on the internet, it is open to the world. Kids need to keep where they live, the school they attend, or any other personal information private.

- **There is healthy and unhealthy screen time.** Like with food, everyone should be mindful regarding screen consumption. There are some great resources on the internet. If they are safe, educational, age-appropriate, and support their development and/or language skills, then it is healthy screen time. However, it is vital to remember that even healthy screen time should have limits. Make sure there are screen-free zones in the house, especially at mealtimes, and when family time is most important in your household.

Social Media Specifics

Social media can be a great way to connect with family and friends, stay informed about important events, and share information.

But we often forget that there are social and developmental skills that are easier for adults and that generally make social media a reasonably positive experience. However, we know that the prefrontal cortex (the part of the brain that allows kids to manage the higher-order thinking skills needed to engage with social media) is not fully developed until we are in our 20s. For example, teenagers may not have the impulse-control skills needed to decide not to post a nasty comment on Facebook or share a revealing photo on Instagram. Just as we teach our kids the appropriate social skills for face-to-face relationships, we also need to teach them social media skills.

When you feel your teenager is ready for social media, as with anything new, there must be rules. However just writing a list and enforcing it won't be effective. Sit down with your child and come up with the rules together. The more you involve them in the process, the more likely it is they will willingly follow them.

- Set rules about WHEN, WHERE, and WITH WHOM your child can use social media. Social media never ends, as there are always notifications and a constant flow of information. These disturbances can make it hard to switch off, and it can be very addictive, so have set times when your teen can be online. You also want to be clear about whom your kids are friends with. You don't want them linking up with strangers, as this opens the door for possible grooming by predators.
- Keep social media out of bedrooms. Research shows that most cyberbullying happens at night (Cross and Walker, 2015). It is thought that this is because, at night, our logical brain (prefrontal cortex) is less active and our emotional/reactional brain (limbic brain) becomes more active. Therefore, we are more likely to say and do things that we might otherwise regret. So, discourage social media use at night.
- Discuss with your children what they share, like, or comment on. Help your child understand the digital footprint they're leaving on social media. It's essential to continue to stay engaged with your child's social media life because you want your child to feel that you're involved. You also want them to know that they can come to you if or when something happens that they don't know how to handle.

143

- It is difficult for children to grasp the magnitude and permanence of social media. Have them ask themselves some questions before they post anything online.

1. Would you be happy if your mum/dad/grandparents/principal saw this post?

2. Would you be willing to stand up in front of a crowd of people and share this post? (This is essentially what happens when something is shared online.)

3. If someone has made a comment that upsets you, take a moment to pause before you respond. When we act out of impulse, we rarely make good decisions.

Social media isn't going away, and for all the negative aspects, there are as many positive ones. But only if we guide our kids. Just like every other learning area in life, it is up to us, as parents, to guide our kids through social media, too.

Given our children are living in a much more advanced technological era, understanding the full impact of social media is hard to grasp. But as we work through it with our children and learn together, we can work toward a positive experience for everyone.

How do we parent our children when they are growing up in a world we have never experienced and we don't know the rules?

@The_Therapist_Parent

Family Screen Time Plan

When looking at your family's online/screen usage, it can be helpful to have a plan. If you take the time to think about what is important to you and your family, it is easier to keep boundaries. Here are some ideas. When you work out what your priorities are, involve your children in what your family rules can be around screens.

When Will There Be Screen Time?

Think about if there will be screen-free times during the day (e.g., at dinner) or screen-free areas in the house. Will you have screen-free 'family time' regularly? What apps/games are okay?

Set and Discuss Digital Safety Rules

Think about how to keep everyone safe. Discuss what can be shared and what to do if there is content that makes someone uncomfortable. Check device security settings. Determine where kids can use screens (e.g. not in bedrooms), who can they 'follow,' and whether their account is private. Have a plan you can put into place if anyone experiences cyberbullying.

What Content Is Good for Your Family?

What content/usage is prioritised? e.g. creative, educational, prosocial, and positive media.

When Your Child Is Being Bullied

When children are together in large groups there is bound to be the odd negative comment or hurtful thing said, but that isn't bullying. Bullying is not one-off negative comments or children being mean about not playing with others on a particular day. Bullying is repeated negative behaviour. It is the ongoing and deliberate actions intended to hurt someone. The bullying may be: physical – hurting someone; verbal – name calling or threats; psychological – spreading rumours; or emotional – deliberately excluding someone. If that wasn't enough, we now also have cyberbullying, where children are taunted on social media or over text or email. This type of bullying is very invasive, as there is no physical break from the bully. They can instantly be in your home, where you are supposed to feel safe.

When parents find out their child is being bullied, they will likely experience waves of emotion. They may want to confront the bully or their parents. They may want to tell their child to punch the bully. Or they could just be completely overwhelmed and not know what to do. Meeting aggression with aggression is not going to help. But we can't just sit by and do nothing.

Our kids need us to help keep them safe. They need us to be their advocate, support, coach, and cheer quad. Some parents take the 'tough love' approach and think that kids should just learn to deal with bullying because it is everywhere. But as an adult, if you were being bullied at your workplace, would you just put up with it? Many people would look for another job and leave. A child doesn't have that sort of power. They are forced to face continued bullying at school, which is supposed to be a safe place.

So, What Can We Do When Our Child Is Being Bullied?

There Is a Line: Firstly, there is never a time when physical violence is okay. A child being hit is assault and should always be dealt with. If your child has been hit or physically hurt, you need to ensure that the school or establishment takes action. You don't need to be aggressive, but you do need to be assertive. Schools have regulations for physical violence, and these need to be followed. While you can teach your child how to handle verbal and emotional bullying (although it should still be reported and dealt with), there should be no tolerance for violence.

146

Bullying of any kind needs to be reported to your school. If the school doesn't act, report the incident to the education department. If it is an ongoing occurrence, then it is bullying, and something needs to be done.

There are strategies you can use to build your child's resilience and assertiveness. Still, if there are continued and deliberate acts to harm your child, then you need to make sure action is taken. Keep a record of the incidents and what steps have been taken. Stay in regular contact with the school principal and teacher. Discuss the plans they have in place and what they are doing to keep your child safe. Devise a strategy your child can implement if something happens. Who should they report to? Are other teachers on the playground and casual staff aware of the bullying? These are important questions to ask and have satisfactorily answered. You need to know that the school is working with you to help anyone being bullied.

Prevention Strategies

If a child feels like negative attention aimed at them may turn into bullying, there are skills we can teach them to help deflect it. Bullying is almost always someone trying to assert power over another. We can teach our kids to develop skills that stop the bully feeling like they have this kind of power in the relationship, hopefully making the bullying pointless.

Have Planned 'Comebacks'

Meeting name-calling with name-calling rarely results in a good outcome. It becomes a war of who can say the nastiest thing, which usually only aggravates the bully and causes them to continue. As crazy as this may seem, agreeing with the bully can be quite effective. Now, when I say agree, I don't mean that you have to believe the horrible things they say about you or you put yourself down. However, when we agree on some level, we take the power out of what the bully is trying to do. For example, if a bully says, "You're so dumb," you could say, "Yeah, I do make mistakes sometimes." Or if they say, "You're ugly," you could say, "Yeah, I'm having a bad hair day." Adding a compliment to the bully can really throw them off. If you add, "You look great, though," they don't really have anywhere else to go. You effectively disarm them. But again, when you tell your kids about this

147

technique, make sure they understand they shouldn't believe what the bully is saying. It is just a technique to find a way to agree with the comment and take away the power.

Humour is a great way to respond to teasing. The problem is, it can be hard to be funny in the moment, especially if you are stressed. It can be helpful to have some comebacks ready if you know you might have to spend time with someone who often teases others. If a bully makes fun of your child missing the ball in a game, they could say, "That's very observant of you," or "Nice of you to notice." If the bully keeps commenting, they could respond, "I wish you wouldn't worry about me so much." Talk to your child about situations that have happened and try to come up with funny comebacks. Come up with as many as you can so your child has lots of 'go-to' things to say.

Role-Play

Many parents cringe at the thought of role-playing with their children, but it is a great way to practise new skills and build your child's confidence to manage challenges. If you role-play, you may see that your child's body language makes them a target. A bully will always target someone they think they can dominate. Have your child practice their comebacks with a strong posture, eye contact (if they are able), and with a firm and confident voice. These non-verbal actions are vital when confronting a bully.

Make a Plan

Talk with your child about what they can do if they need help. Who are they confident will help them? Which friends can play nearby? Are there teachers they feel comfortable talking to? Involve your child in planning a range of alternatives and have them problem-solve each option. You also need to explain to your child that your job is to keep them safe, and if you feel that it has gone too far, you will ensure that the school deals with it properly.

Build Resilience

One of the most powerful ways a child builds resilience is through the unwavering knowledge that their parents or carers love and accept them for who they are. They need to know your love for them will never change, no matter what they experience or how they react. Knowing this provides assurance that they are worthwhile and valued. However, if a child has experienced extended periods of bullying, even this will begin to erode.

As kids get older, they need more than just their parent's acceptance. They need people around them who 'get' them. They need friends. Having friends that share similar interests and ideals is vital when it comes to resilience. This way, it is not as detrimental if someone (the bully) doesn't like you. At least you have others who do. The bully's opinion simply doesn't matter as much when you have a group of people who support you.

Finding friends, however, can be challenging. Kids are expected to get along just because they attend the same school, and that simply isn't enough reason to be friends. Really knowing yourself is the cornerstone of making friends. But this is hard for kids. They are just learning what they like and what they are good at. You can work with your child to find their strengths and encourage this knowledge to empower them. And remember, friends don't have to be at school. They could be at scouts, in art classes, or on sports teams. As parents, we need to support these friendships by organising playdates or phone calls and maintaining accessibility to keep their bonds strong.

Coping with bullying is hard for everyone. No parent wants to see their child bullied, and it can be hard to know what to do. Remembering that it is our job to keep our kids safe can help us take the necessary action. Work with the school to help support our kids while in their care, and coach, support, and encourage them to become assertive and resilient.

There are many factors that build (resilience.) We aren't just born with it. At the core of resilience is having the assurance that you are (loved) for who you are no matter what

@The_Therapist_Parent

Bullying - Make a Plan

First of all, if there is bullying within the school, the school needs to know about it. They have a duty of care to keep children safe while at school. Start with your child's teacher, then the department head, and the principal. If you aren't satisfied with how the bullying is being managed, go to the education department.

The strategies below can be used by your child if they are safe and the bullying can be managed. These give your child some tools so they don't feel helpless, but if the bullying has continued, then action needs to be taken.

Planned Comebacks

Some people are great at comebacks, but when you are stressed it is hard to think and come up with anything. It is good to have some on hand. You can use these or come up with some yourself. Try not to be mean, as that will only antagonise the bully. We want to disarm them, not fire them up. If you can make your comment positive, it will take the bully by surprise.

- You're giving me a lot of your attention, I'm flattered.
- You have mistaken me for someone who cares.
- The amount of time you waste on me, if you spend it on your life, you will do great.
- That's strange, I don't remember asking for your opinion.
- Did that make you feel good? Awesome, glad to be of service, you can thank me later.
- Wow, good try.
- We must have a lot in common then.
- Really? I think you are great.
- Not everyone can be a winner like you.

What are your ideas?

Sometimes, just a confused look and shaking your head is enough. Have your child practise their comebacks with a strong posture, eye contact (if they are able), and with a firm and confident voice. These non-verbal actions are vital when confronting a bully.

<u>Make a plan</u>

Make sure your child knows what to do if things go too far. Who can they speak to? Who are the trusted adults? Where is it safest in the playground?

Everyday Resilience

As a psychologist, I often hear people say, "That child just lacks resilience." This is an unfair comment to make. Sometimes, such a reaction has more to do with an adult not wanting to deal with a child's feelings than the child's resilience. However, resilience is something we want our children to develop. We don't want them to get washed by the waves of life and hope they can rise above their hardships, because nobody is immune from difficult times. It is up to us to help our children grow and develop these skills.

Just because a child gets upset doesn't mean they aren't resilient; there is much more to it than that. Resilience is the ability to persevere through difficulties. It's not the absence of ever getting upset; when you're resilient, you just don't stay caught in overwhelm. The problem isn't that you're feeling the emotions; it's that you don't have the skills to handle them without being overwhelmed. This is why a child needs a parent or connected adult in their life. The secure relationship and solid bond they share allow the child to co-regulate, and eventually learn to self-regulate. With this guidance, kids learn that we all experience heightened emotions and that feelings do pass, no matter how intense they might be at the time. They also come to understand that with support, they can calm themselves and move on. However, when we leave children overwhelmed by strong emotions, they never learn how to move through them. Instead, they learn ways to avoid these emotions, not try scary things, avoid mistakes, and ultimately have poor resilience. A parent's relationship with their child is the cornerstone of that child's resilience.

Resilience isn't innate; it's learned and grown through experience. Part of resilience is knowing you can 'do hard things.' Children must face difficulties, mistakes, and failures to understand they can overcome them. We can't expect them to have this trait without the experiences that builds it. Even small challenges, like losing a game or not going first, are valuable experiences for them. These 'little things' are their stepping stones to resilience. When children feel secure in their safety, connection, and emotions, they'll be more willing to take healthy risks and not fear falling short. They learn that mistakes and disappointments are not the end but opportunities for growth, and they become curious, brave, and develop trust in themselves.

Their everyday experiences help teach them this. Exhausting, frustrating moments of upset are exactly what children need for resilience, but they need our help to realise this.

What Can We Do?

When a child is overwhelmed, try these steps:

Calm

Returning a child to a calm state is always the first step, as this allows them to access the logical part of their brain. They can't move through the emotion if they are completely overwhelmed by it. Remember, young children need your help to calm, so stay close, offer hugs, and support them through it.

Wait

Wait out the emotions with your child. Don't jump in and try to fix the situation or rush them. It is necessary to feel the emotion rise to experience it fully, avoid distracting ourselves from the feeling, and come through the other side safely. While waiting, validate your child's feelings so they know you understand.

Help

Assist them to think flexibly and avoid merely reacting to the situation. However, only do this once they are calm. Jumping in with assistance too early will only make them feel like you don't understand, and it can reactivate the emotion. This is why validating their feelings is so important. Also, help them see if they are using extreme words like 'always' and 'never,' as this can exacerbate the permanence they feel about the situation. If they can shift their thinking slightly, it can improve how they feel.

Find Solutions

Work together to come up with possibilities for the situation. When we support children and let them come up with ideas, we help build their self-esteem and the confidence to manage setbacks. Having children think through different scenarios will also help develop executive functioning (planning, focusing attention, remembering, and doing more than one thing at a time).

Make a Helpful Mindset Part of Every Day

Children as young as five can understand the principles of positive thinking (Bamford and Laguttuta, 2011). They understand that a positive thought helps you feel better, and a negative thought makes you feel worse. Our mindset is important, as is being able to change it when we realise we have become stuck in a negative gear; this is the opposite of resilience.

Being careful with your own thoughts is a high priority because children pick up on your attitude. It is easy, as parents, to use permanent language such as, "You always leave your toys on the floor" or, "You never flush the toilet." While it may feel that way, these are probably extreme thoughts born of frustration rather than the reality of the situation. Children take in how we look at the world when we speak like this. The more optimistic we can be, the better children grow to understand the benefits of a helpful mindset.

Do your best to consciously see things positively in your own life and comment about it. Point out how your children can look for the good in their situations, too; e.g., before the first day of the school year, you could say, "Tomorrow is your first day! What are you looking forward to?" If they feel anxious, help them change the focus of their thoughts; "Yes, it is hard when things are new. What might happen that you will enjoy?" The earlier a child learns to think like this, the easier it will be as they get older. Remember, helpful thinking doesn't mean dismissing the negatives. Acknowledge this perspective, but help your child see what else is true that helps them feel better.

Self-Awareness

Children who are self-aware see themselves as uniquely different from other people. They start to know their own minds, feelings, bodies, and sensations, ultimately leading to better emotional awareness and a positive outlook. To help with this, look for times when your child feels good about themselves and help them recognise their thoughts and feelings. What feels good to them? Tell them what you noticed about them. If children become aware of when they feel good, they will look for these moments and therefore will experience them more often.

155

Gratitude

A gratitude practice improves helpful thinking and, therefore, resilience. When we start looking for the good, it allows us to focus on optimism and gratitude. Talk about what makes you smile, your favourite memories, and what brings you joy. Make sure to help your child see that these don't have to be big things; simply enjoying the feeling of the sun on your skin, the smell of spring, or whatever currently brings a smile to their face is enough to bring a sense of gratitude.

Our level of resilience impacts us throughout our lives, ebbing and flowing with life's circumstances and abilities. We are not born resilient; it is something that each person must develop, and the best thing we can do for our children is to help them fully develop theirs. We must stay connected with our children, work through emotions, model a helpful mindset, and look for moments of gratitude throughout the day. Difficult days might be challenging, but they are also the best training ground to build resilience.

When helping a child through disappointment and big emotions

Validate the feeling

Support them through till the wave passes

@The_Therapist_Parent

Come up with a plan together

Then

Building Resilience When Things Don't Work Out as Planned

No parent likes seeing their child hurting. We would do just about anything to save them from pain. But disappointment, frustration, and mistakes are something everyone needs to experience and learn to deal with well. We often want to walk our kids quickly through these uncomfortable emotions, distract them, or buy them something to make them feel better. Our logical, developed brain wants to tell them that it's not a big deal and to find a solution. But when we don't allow our kids to go through the process, we are robbing them of developing resilience and, ultimately, confidence that they can overcome or at least survive setbacks.

So, how do we not feel completely defeated as parents when watching our children suffer? It isn't easy, but if we help our kids when they are young, they will be better equipped to handle setbacks in adult life.

Validate the Feeling and Wait

When something happens that upsets your child, don't be in a rush to move them through it, as uncomfortable as that may sound. Acknowledge the negative feelings or that the situation doesn't feel fair. Don't try to sugar-coat it; sometimes, things are just really disappointing. Let them talk, cry, or whatever they need; just be there for them for as long as it takes. Don't try to fix anything. Calmly sit and listen.

As parents, this waiting can be incredibly hard. We want to 'fix' the situation and make it better. But for the sake of your child's future resilience, just wait. Wait until they are ready; they need to know that hard emotions do pass. If we never allow kids to experience the full wave of an emotion, then these feelings can end up becoming very scary things.

Be careful not to dismiss their feelings as 'silly' or 'no big deal.' This only causes them to believe their feelings are unimportant and that you don't fully appreciate their situation; you don't 'get it.' This makes them feel more isolated, taking them into a downward spiral of difficult and damaging emotions. It might be something as simple as drawing out of the lines, but to them, in that moment, it is a big deal. Let them know that you understand and will support them. If we can do this, the feelings will have the opportunity to pass. We don't need to shut them down.

Share a Similar Experience

It is important to be careful when we share our experiences. The idea is to help your child understand that you have been through similar things and that you appreciate what it feels like. This is not an opportunity to 'outdo' them. Don't try to make their disappointment feel small in comparison to yours; their situation is not about you. However, if you have been through something similar, then it can be helpful for them to realise that they aren't the only one to have such an experience. By sharing a time when you felt the same way, you can connect with them through that emotion. If you have never been through anything like what your child is going through, then let them know that you can imagine how it must feel.

Praise the Effort

It is so important for our kids to know that even if they 'fail' at something, your love will not be affected. If they are disappointed because they didn't make it through an audition or a test that they tried hard to do well in, then make sure you shift the focus to the effort and the bravery that it took in the first place. They need to know that you see more than the end result, and their character is what matters.

Role Model Disappointment

Kids are always watching, and we can use this to our advantage. When we are disappointed, make a mistake, or plans don't work out as we had hoped, let them see. Explain how you feel when an appointment gets changed, or a meeting with your friends is cancelled. But also let them see and hear your problem-solving process. Speak about what you can do, and how you try to cope. Obviously, don't do this with big worries; kids don't need to take on adult concerns. But you may as well let them hear you working things out in a positive way. They are watching anyway.

We need kids to see that disappointments and mistakes are a part of life. We all go through them. But what matters is how we move through the disappointment to results that often turn out to be powerful learning experiences. When you make a mistake, practise saying things like, "Oh well, we all make mistakes, that's how we learn." Let them see you giving yourself grace and the freedom to mess things up sometimes.

Come Up with a Plan

Don't move to this step too quickly. Be guided by your child as to when they feel ready to think of a way through the problem. When they have moved through the difficult emotions, they are better positioned to determine the cause. From there, they can see if there is anything they can do and also begin to think about how to avoid such a situation in the future. Disappointment can be a great motivator if we let it.

Work with your child to determine what the problem was. Teach them to look at mistakes with a curious eye and to ask questions, such as: "What would you like to change?" "What could you add to the situation?" Focus on what they can do instead of what they can't. Was there anything they could have done? If not, does this change how they feel about the situation? Perhaps they could gain enough insight to make a plan to get through next time.

Get them to consider how they have overcome disappointments in the past and what skills you have noticed that they could use again. Offer suggestions, but as much as possible, try and let them work out what to do. You want them to develop this skill, not feel they have to ask someone else to solve their problems every time they arise. Just support them and think through the plans with them. If you don't think the plan will work, ask questions such as, "What might happen if we did that?"

If their disappointment is not something that they want to improve, then work toward finding their strengths. We aren't good at everything, but everyone is good at or passionate about something. It can be helpful for children to realise that it is okay not to be good at some things. We can't all be good runners or great singers. Help them find what they are good at and follow goals for that.

Whether it is missing a key while playing the piano, not getting picked for a sporting team, colouring out of the lines, or not doing well in a test, we must support our children through these uncomfortable times and see them as the teaching opportunities they are. It is a time to validate and move through the emotions and then support our children to eventually see that learning will come. Above all, when things don't go as planned, we can show our children that they are loved as they learn and grow.

159

When children have a "bad day" they can feel so overwhelmed and very alone. They don't understand that we all feel like that sometimes and feelings do change

Resilience Building Activities

'Mistake' Art

Helping children see that it's okay to make mistakes is an important step in building their resilience. A fun and effective way to do this is by making 'mistake' art. They can problem-solve by thinking of alternative ways to be creative.

To make 'mistake art', you'll need:

- Paper
- Markers
- Coloured pencils
- Crayons
- Paint and paintbrushes (optional)

Step 1: Give them a piece of paper and let them choose which art supplies they'd like to draw with.

Step 2: Have them to close their eyes and draw something. It might be as simple as a circle or some parallel lines.

Step 3: Once they've done the first part with their eyes closed, remind them that it's okay to make mistakes. Instead of starting over and trying to draw the thing perfectly, they can come up with ways to turn what they have done into something creative. If they're unsure of what to do, you can make suggestions but try to help them come up with something.

Make a Boat (Or Any Craft)

Building a mini boat with twigs and leaves can be tricky. There's plenty of opportunity for frustration. Learning to cope when things go wrong is exactly what we want to help build resilience. When the frustration starts, help your child to recognise their feelings, take a deep breath, look at their thoughts, and try something else. In the end, it doesn't really matter how wonky it is – focus on the effort and the ability to keep going when things don't go to plan.

Letting Kids Be Bored Can Be Constructive

"I'm bored." The two words that make every parent cringe and sigh, especially when it comes from a child surrounded by an array of toys and other things specifically chosen to amuse them. Somehow, a culture has developed that expects parents to keep children entertained and happy. This stems from the belief that parents aren't doing enough if their kids are bored. When actually, the opposite is true. It is good for our kids to experience boredom. When we swoop in and entertain them, we stop them from problem-solving, becoming creative, and ultimately building resilience. That doesn't mean they should be put in a bare room with nothing to do because 'boredom is good for them.' Boredom with no options can lead to frustration, which is not beneficial at all. However, the type of boredom that is beneficial is what researchers have labelled "constructive boredom" (Gasper and Middlewood, 2013).

Constructive boredom occurs when children are given opportunities to be creative without structure or direction. For example, you may suggest that children use a cardboard box and craft material but not tell them what to make or how to make it. The benefits of this type of boredom come when kids are allowed to have some control over what they do. They are challenged and must solve their own problems. It is the opposite of over-scheduling activities or turning to screens that flood their brains with stimulation (and not much else).

Have you ever noticed that when you do something mundane, you start to daydream? That's when you come up with the most amazing ideas. Research confirms that when we experience a certain amount of boredom, we become more creative thinkers (Richardson, 2013). Children become incredibly resourceful when they are bored if they are in an environment that supports creativity. This is when children write and act out plays in the backyard, make magic potions from mud and leaves, craft spaceships from egg cartons, or build the most amazing Lego creations. When they work through boredom, children learn to manage failures and come up with ideas to make things work, and this is where they build their self-esteem, when they can see what they have created.

As you can see, constructive boredom inspires creativity, builds autonomy, provides problem-solving opportunities, and ultimately supports self-esteem and resilience. So, how do we create opportunities for creative boredom?

Make a Creative List: I sit down with my kids every school holiday to brainstorm what they would like to do during the break. They can have a few external activities, like going to the movies or a café, but we try to come up with creative ideas they can do at home. Thinking ahead in this way ensures I have time to prepare everything needed for the chosen activities. In addition, having these ideas written down is the perfect reference tool for when the kids say, "I'm bored." They have a ready-made list of ideas they have created themselves. This approach encourages autonomy by allowing kids the freedom to choose what they do. As each activity is completed, they tick it off, providing a sense of achievement. As a result of this small amount of planning, we never find that the holidays just slip by like nothing really happened.

Some ideas you might like to include (that were especially popular when my kids were around four and six years old): go fishing, find a pet caterpillar, play cricket together, go to the park, do some gardening, go to a café, learn to tie shoelaces, and cook and toast marshmallows on the fire.

Be as creative as you like. The most important part of this activity is to allow your child to come up with ideas and let them have some responsibility for how they will spend their time.

Have Resources Available: You know your child and what they like and dislike. If they don't like drawing, it won't matter how many art supplies you buy; it won't help when they are bored. Find the things they love and have them available. If it is sports, make sure that their football isn't flat. If it is Lego, ensure you haven't sucked it all up the vacuum. If it is cooking, then have the ingredients for their favourite recipes. We can't expect kids to pull something out of nothing. We do have to set up the environment for them, but then let them run with it.

Where Possible, Be Out in Nature: Being outside provides so many opportunities it is hard to stay bored. There are bugs to find, trees to climb, sticks to turn into magic wands, or you can simply lay on the grass and imagine pictures in the clouds.

My kids have stopped saying, "I'm bored," because my reaction is always, "Fantastic! I wonder what creative things you will come up with." Unsurprisingly, this is usually followed by some eye rolling and a good laugh.

While we should be there to offer suggestions and help when things become too difficult, ultimately, the benefits of letting children feel some boredom are well worth the small amount of discomfort.

Trying to entertain and keep children happy all the time

Inhibits creativity and emotion regulation

Parental burnout

@The_Therapist_Parent

School Holiday Activity List

Sit down together before the school holidays and come up with some ideas your children would like to do. As much as possible, try to think of things that don't cost a lot of money and can be done at home. Here are a few ideas, play café with real food, look for bugs, roast marshmallows, make a fort, painting, face painting, cooking, gardening.

Activity	What do we need?	Tick when done

Why Children Need to Do Chores

One of parents' biggest complaints is that their children don't help out around the house. It can feel like a constant battle. So should we bother? Surely, it is just easier to do the tasks ourselves? Well, the answer is "Yes" to both questions. It might be easier just to do the jobs ourselves, initially. But the research is overwhelming and Dr Kennedy-Moore (2013) reports that adults who did chores as children are happier and more successful.

Having help around the house is not the most important advantage of getting your kids to do chores. It impacts their self-esteem, gives them a sense of responsibility, and helps them feel like valued and trusted members of the family when they are required to do tasks. It also provides opportunities for them to manage frustration and take pride in their achievements. It's hard to believe that all of these benefits can be attributed to making a bed, cleaning a room, and taking out the rubbish. But it is true. In addition, as children get older and are given more responsibility, they develop essential life skills and independence.

When we let children help us or they do chores independently, it is important that we recognise their effort and show appreciation. "Thank you for picking up the toys – that was such a big help!" Focus on what they did and their effort, rather than saying, "Good work" or, "Good kid." Emphasising their ability and effort is more important than a focus on what they did. Teach them how to do the chore, and then let them do it on their own. When you show confidence in your child's abilities, they will build confidence in themselves. When they put in effort and eventually succeed, they will have a sense of achievement, which is a great reward.

So, When Can Children Start Doing Chores?

It can be difficult to know what you should expect your children to do and at what age. However, children as young as three can do basic chores. We just have to get our expectations right. You can't expect a three-year-old to put their clothes away in the correct drawers or completely clean their rooms themselves. However, they can pack their toys away and help you with other simple chores. In the same way, teenagers should be doing more than just getting their dirty clothes to the laundry.

We have to get the balance between ability and expectation right and also remember that they might need some help sometimes.

Now, every child develops differently. What one child can do will be different from another of the same age. But to give a rough guide, the following is a list of general household chores that most children can do at each age. I'm not suggesting that they do these everyday or all of them on the list, but they are some possibilities you could work out as a family.

Age Three
- Help make their bed.
- Pick up toys with your supervision.
- Take their dirty clothes to the laundry basket.
- Fill a pet's water and food bowls (with supervision).
- Help a parent clean up spills and dirt.

Ages Four and Five
- Get dressed with minimal help.
- Make their bed with minimal help.
- Put their bag and shoes away.
- Set the table with supervision.
- Clear the table with supervision.
- Help a parent prepare food.
- Help a parent carry in the lighter groceries.
- Match clean socks.
- Be responsible for a pet's food and water bowl.
- Hang up towels in the bathroom.

Ages Six and Seven
- Make their bed.
- Get dressed and ready for the day.
- Be responsible for a pet's food and water.
- Put their laundry in their drawers.
- Put away dishes from the dishwasher.
- Help prepare food with supervision.

167

Ages Eight to 11

- Shower, clean teeth themselves.
- Keep bedroom clean.
- Be responsible for homework.
- Wake up using an alarm clock (if they want to).
- Wash dishes, stack, and unstack the dishwasher.
- Wash the family car with help.
- Clean the bathroom with help.
- Learn to use the washer and dryer.
- Put all laundry away.
- Pack lunches.
- Take rubbish out.

Ages 12 and 13

- Take care of personal hygiene, belongings, and homework.
- Set their alarm clock.
- Maintain personal items, such as recharging batteries.
- Change bed sheets.
- Keep their room tidy and clean.
- Dust, vacuum, clean bathrooms, and do dishes.
- Mow the lawn with supervision.
- Prepare an occasional family meal.

Ages 14 and 15

- Responsible for all personal chores for ages 12 and 13.
- Responsible for library card and books.
- Do assigned housework without prompting.
- Do gardening work as needed.
- Prepare food — from making a grocery list and buying the items (with supervision) to serving a meal — occasionally.

Ages 16 to 18

- Responsible for all personal chores for ages 14 and 15.
- Responsible for earning spending money.
- Do housework as needed.
- Do gardening work as needed.
- Prepare family meals — from grocery list to serving — as needed.

So, How Do We Get Them to Do These Chores?

Well, this is not always easy. But you are more likely to get compliance from children if you give them some control and choice. However, cleaning up after themselves is not an extra chore. This is just learning to be responsible for themselves, and they need to do this, regardless.

1. Sit down as a family with a list of all the chores that need to be done in your household. You may have to explain why and how often these things need to be done. A child may not understand that a bathroom needs to be cleaned regularly, or mould and bacteria can build up.

2. Give your kids choices about the chores they are willing to do. They need to commit to these jobs.

3. Agreement on how often these should be done and when. Some things must be done daily, but you can negotiate when they do them.

4. Be clear about whether children are expected to remember to do the chore independently, or if you will remind them to do the job. Some things, like putting their dirty clothes in the laundry, will be expected without reminders, but you might remind them to clean the bathroom.

This is also an excellent time to discuss any difficulties you have had getting them to do the chore in the past. Brainstorm together about what they could do to avoid arguments or having to be nagged. A chart that they can tick off completed jobs can be helpful. I'm not suggesting a reward-based chart, just a visual reminder (like a to-do list) where they can see what they need to do on which days. Give them a chance to contribute ideas too. Nobody likes arguing, and they may have suggestions to avoid this outcome.

169

Whatever chores you decide are best for your family are up to you. The responsibility that comes with doing household duties is far more important than the task itself. Along with making life easier and strengthening family ties, working together will help your children develop the skills they need to succeed well into the future.

Reminder Chart

A chart to tick off completed jobs can be helpful. I'm not suggesting a reward-based chart, just a visual reminder (like a to-do list) where they can see what they need to do on which days. Here is an example.

TO DO	MONDAY	TUESDAY	WEDNESDAY
MORNING			
AFTERNOON			
NIGHT			
EXTRA			

If your child has forgotten to do a chore, instead of saying, "Go and do..." you can direct them to look at the chart and see where they are up to. This gives them independence and helps them to plan ahead. Don't turn the chart into a fight, it is just a reminder. If they are having trouble following it, have a conversation about why it isn't working. Be curious and see if there are any changes you could make.

5.

Caring for Ourselves

When Parents Burn Out

I always advocate looking for positives, being grateful, and challenging negative thinking. These skills definitely improve our mood and build resilience, but we also need to know when we are drained and heading towards 'burnout.'

Studies have shown that when parents suffer burnout, they, ironically, become the parents they would prefer to avoid. In this situation, mums and dads often want distance from their children in an attempt to restore themselves. Unfortunately, this damages the relationships around them and causes more parenting struggles. The struggles then compound feelings of burnout, and the pattern continues. The study also found that parental burnout can eventually lead to parental abuse and neglect (Mikolajczak et al, 2019.)

To help our children manage their emotions, they need a calm adult to co-regulate and work through the difficulties with them. We all know that our tolerance levels are low when we have had very little sleep or are at 'breaking point' from over-commitment. In these situations, we become just as reactive as our kids and end up modelling the behaviour that we desperately want them to STOP.

What is Burnout?

Burnout is a state of emotional, mental, and often physical exhaustion brought on by prolonged or repeated stress. The stress can come from any source; work, relationships, or day-to-day parenting. The problem isn't the intensity of the pressure. It is the duration. When you feel like there is no end, you can only last so long before you burn out.

The symptoms of burnout can vary. Most research relates to work-related stress, but there are some common symptoms that you may notice:

Exhaustion: Burnout brings intense exhaustion that no amount of sleep seems to cure. With it often comes a heaviness that doesn't seem to leave. The fatigue seems to fill every part of your being; physical, mental, and emotional.

Low Motivation/Energy: Your willingness to do things disappears. Activities that you used to do with enthusiasm now seem too hard. A personal example of this was Christmas recently.

I have always loved Christmas. I love decorating and buying or making presents. I love everything about it. But Christmas just seemed too hard. I had to make myself put up the tree, and I found myself wishing for it to be over.

Becoming Frustrated and Cynical: When we are at our limit with stress, our tolerance for other things decreases. You may snap at people more often or your view of the world might becomes darker. It is okay to have days like this, but if there is a prolonged change in your mood, then you are likely burned out.

Reduced Productivity: Low motivation tends to result in only doing the bare minimum you have to. This can be with work, but it can also be with relationships and parenting. When you don't have the emotional energy for yourself, it is tough to help your child regulate theirs.

Reduced Compassion: When we are depleted, there is literally nothing left to give anyone else. It isn't that we don't care. It is just that we can't spare any compassion for others. A numbness can come with burnout; what once evoked a response now just passes us by.

These symptoms seem very similar to depression. However, there are a few critical differences. Depression usually also includes poor self-esteem, intense hopelessness, and possibly, suicidal thoughts. Depression is a serious condition that needs to be treated by a professional. If you feel that you could be suffering from depression, please see your doctor. There is a lot that can be done to help.

So, what do we do if we are heading towards burnout or are already there? Quite simply, you need to do what helps you feel restored, which will be different for everyone. A holiday is great, but that is only a short-term solution. You need to put regular habits in place that help you feel better and reduce the chance of burning out again. If something fills your cup, do it, because this will ultimately help you. As a result of feeling restored, everyone around you benefits, too.

There is another benefit of practising self-care. By modelling care for ourselves, we teach our children that they need to care for themselves as well. We show that it is okay to say "No" to things when feeling overwhelmed, that eating well and exercising are essential, and that we all need to do something that 'light us up' to make life enjoyable.

As self-care has the same mental and physical effects on your child's health as ours, we should definitely encourage and model it. After all, we want our kids to grow into adults who can set boundaries, have healthy relationships, and can care for themselves physically and emotionally.

Burnout Prevention

Self-Care: Find what helps you feel restored rather than depleted, and do it. What makes one person feel refuelled may not work for another. If you are not sure, try different things and notice the impact they have. Layering mindfulness and gratitude over your self-care rituals will always enhance their benefits.

Restore Focus: Often, it isn't what we are doing that causes burnout. It is just the constant drudgery that seems to suck the life out of us. If we take some time to sit back and remember why we are doing what we are doing, it can help us find our lost motivation. Constant parenting, managing emotional outbursts, teaching, and guiding is exhausting. But when we realise that our goal is to raise emotionally stable people, we remember the purpose of it all. If work or other commitments have sent you on the road to burnout, take the time to discover why you are doing them. Do you still have the same goals and values? Can you more closely align the purpose behind your actions, or do you need to find a new way to do things?

Find a Passion: When you are burned out, you need to reignite the fire somehow. This doesn't necessarily mean a new job; it might be finding a new hobby or interest. What do you love, and how can you do it more? If you are burned out, you will probably have limited motivation even for this, but do what you can. Do what you have always loved and see if it restores you to who you know you really are.

Burnout can create a downward spiral if action is not taken. We can't be empathetic and patient parents if we are stressed and overwhelmed. This can cause us to feel guilty, and down we go! Taking care of ourselves helps us be the best parents we can be, teaches our kids the importance of self-care, and empowers them with coping strategies for life.

Parental Burnout's
Downward Spiral

High Expectations

Doing Everything for Everyone

No time for self-care

Exhausted

Tolerance Drops

Lose temper

Guilt

negative thinking

@The__Therapist__Parent

Burnout

Self-Care is Not Selfish

It can seem to many parents that the world's pressures amplify from the moment their tiny baby comes into the world. A typical parent struggles with a lack of sleep, financial stress, juggling work and child care, worries about their child's health and development, increased housework, and a general lack of time for oneself. This lifestyle can leave us feeling completely depleted. The problem is, when we don't care for ourselves, we can't be the effective parents we want to be.

We know that helping our children manage their emotions requires a calm adult who can regulate with them and work through the difficulties together. We also know that our tolerance levels are low when we have had very little sleep or are at 'breaking point' from overcommitment. In these circumstances, we can become just as reactive as our kids and end up modelling the behaviour we desperately want them to STOP.

Self-care has many personal benefits, but one of the greatest comes when we model this behaviour. When our children see us caring for ourselves, we teach them that they, too, need to care for themselves.

We can show them that it is okay to say "No" to commitments when you are feeling overwhelmed, that you need to eat well and exercise, and that we all need to do things that 'light us up,' as this makes life enjoyable.

Self-care can have the same effect on maintaining your child's mental and physical health as it does for you. After all, we want our kids to grow into adults who know how to set boundaries, have healthy relationships, and can care for themselves physically and emotionally.

What is Self-Care?

Self-care is more than just bubble baths and manicures, although these can be good, too. Self-care is anything that helps us feel restored, as opposed to those things that leave us feeling depleted. What makes one person feel 'refuelled' will be different from another. For some, having the house tidy is really important, and they prioritise this. For others, it's having time to be creative and paint or do craft. It really is different for everyone.

However, there are general categories that self-care seems to fit into, and they encompass any activity that we do or don't do deliberately to take care of our physical, mental, and emotional health.

Physical Self-Care

It is essential not to neglect the basics. Sleep, eating well, exercising, and having regular health checks are often overlooked when it comes to self-care. But if our bodies aren't functioning at their best, how do we expect to be able to do everything we need to do?

We don't need much convincing that sleep is essential. We all know how hard it is to function when we have had a difficult night. The truth is, sleep is as important to our health as eating and drinking. It allows our bodies to repair themselves and our brains to consolidate memories and process information. Poor sleep is linked to physical problems, such as a weakened immune system and mental health problems, such as anxiety and depression (Scott et al, 2021). So, when we choose to stop Netflix from playing the next episode and make ourselves go to bed, we are actually choosing to care for ourselves and prioritise our health.

The same is true when we eat healthily most of the time (although sometimes self-care includes indulging). In making this choice, we recognise that we are important and deserve to treat our bodies well.

When it comes to exercise, it doesn't have to be boot camp at 5am. Unless this is something that you enjoy, of course. But exercise is important, and as good for our emotional health as it is for our physical health. It increases serotonin levels, which leads to improved mood and energy (Stanton et al, 2014). But again, what's important is choosing a form of exercise you like. A walk, Pilates, running, riding a bike, sport, it doesn't matter. You just have to keep moving and give yourself permission to make this time a priority.

Physical Self-Care for Kids

Obviously, it will depend on your child's age and what they are capable of, but introducing physical self-care is important. It could be as simple as blowing their nose by themselves, brushing their teeth, or understanding that we must wash our hands before eating. We can explain that it is essential to look after our bodies, and by doing these things, children are doing what is required to stay healthy.

It is often difficult to get children to eat their vegetables. But if we teach them to understand its importance for their health, we can set them on the right path. Please don't force children to eat vegetables, as this will only cause them to associate these foods with a negative experience. But continue to serve vegetables and encourage them to keep trying them. Most importantly, you need to eat them, too. Let them see you eat and enjoy them.

When it comes to teaching kids to maintain physical health, there are many ways to encourage good habits. You can exercise together in a lot of different, fun ways, like kicking a ball in the backyard. The important thing isn't necessarily to get into great shape or to take on big athletic challenges, but to build a regular routine of physical self-care that maintains good health and balance. Talk to them about how good it feels after doing some exercise and help them notice how their body feels.

Mental Self-Care

Parenting can be incredibly mentally overwhelming. There are so many things to think about and remember. That's why one of the best ways to care for our mental health is to learn to say "No." We must recognise which of our boundaries help us cope and stick to them. This might mean not answering the phone during dinner, not emailing between certain times of the day, or saying "No" to extra commitments. It could even mean having a weekend without going anywhere if you and your family need some 'downtime.'

On the other hand, you could be someone who recharges by going out with your friends. If you feel 'human' again after a night out with your friends, then this is your clue that you need to make time for these activities. You may not need a night out every week. It could just be a coffee date, a phone call, or another way to feel connected. Work out what you need, how often you need it, and then make it a priority.

Mental Self-Care for Kids

Identifying and expressing feelings is something that needs to be learned, and this can be acquired as early as age three. Helping children to verbalise emotions is as simple as teaching 'feeling words.' Discussing the characters' emotions in your

178

child's favourite stories is a great way to do this. Have fun engaging in this way with your kids. You can even encourage them to draw how they are feeling.

These simple strategies benefit your child's social relationships and help-seeking behaviours. Children who use emotion-related words have been found to have less difficulty making friends. The ability to use words to express emotions gives young children a valuable tool to support their mental health.

Emotional Self-Care

When understanding mindfulness, we know that stopping and being present can help us to move from an emotionally stressed state to an emotionally calm place. But this doesn't mean we have to sit for hour-long meditations. It can be as simple as teaching ourselves to stop and appreciate where we are.

Learning to relax and calm ourselves benefits every aspect of our lives. You could do this with a few minutes of slow, controlled breathing. Having a gratitude journal could help you to reflect on the positive experiences in your life. Or, it could be getting up before anyone else in the morning and appreciating the peace and quiet.

Emotional Self-Care for Kids

Make 'downtime' a priority. Everyone can benefit from some time without the high pressure of activities or the over-stimulation of screens. Make a space in your routine for a regular time when your child can choose a quiet activity they enjoy; drawing, playing with Lego, making craft, or playing a board game are good choices. Such quiet activities help children feel calm and provide the time and space to decompress and regulate their emotional states.

It is always a good idea to teach your children relaxation and mindfulness (see page 191 for more ideas). It can help to do something together so they see that you benefit, too.

A lack of self-care can create a downward spiral (see page 175). If we are stressed and overwhelmed, being empathetic and patient parents is incredibly difficult. This can then cause us to feel guilty – and down we go. Taking care of ourselves helps us to be the best parent we can be. On top of this, it teaches our kids the importance of self-care and models coping strategies for life.

Sometimes Self-Care is doing More (Not) less

@The_Therapist_Parent

Self-Care Activities

As parents, self-care has to be one our most neglected needs, but it is quite possibly the most important. Caring for children is draining in every sense of the word. But to be able to parent at our best and model the behaviour that we want to see in our children, we have to look after ourselves. It is a simple fact, but so hard to do. We often get overwhelmed by the idea of looking after ourselves as well, we are just so busy looking after everyone else. If we start with just the basics, then look at our physical, mental, and emotional needs, it can be less overwhelming. Just adding a few small changes can make a world of difference.

Here are some ideas. Have a look and see which would work for you.

Basics

It's hard to even think of these as self-care because they are such basic needs, but they are also often the most neglected.

Sleep: Having a regular bedtime will really help your body get into a good sleep routine. It is very difficult when you have young children waking through the night. As much as you can, try to make sleep a priority.

Water: It is so easy when you are busy to forget to drink. Try having a water bottle around so you can keep track of how much you are drinking.

Nutrition: Parents often have a diet of eating the crusts off their kid's plates or whatever else is quick and easy. We can't function well if our blood sugar levels rise and crash all day. If you can't sit and eat a proper lunch, make sure you have some healthy snack foods on hand. Nuts, fruit, boiled eggs, leftover dinner, etc. are all good choices.

Medical Checks: Many of us make sure the kids see the dentist, optometrist, etc. but don't make time for ourselves. We need to change our view on this. Our kids need us healthy, and making time for appointments is part of us staying well.

Exercise: There will be quite a few of us that will groan when we think of exercise. We all know it is good for us, but it takes time and energy, something that most parents don't have a lot of. But it is really important, and if you make the time for it, you will feel the difference. The key is finding something you enjoy and can fit into your lifestyle. It could be a 20-minute Pilates session on YouTube in the morning, a couple of 10-minute walks during the day, or a run in the afternoon. It doesn't have to be a lot, but if you specifically make time for it, you will be more likely to do it.

What basic changes will you make?

Mental

Mental self-care focuses on managing everything that goes on in our head. From our mental load, to our internal dialog, and keeping ourselves mentally stimulated. All too often we are carrying the mental load for everyone in the family and, eventually, something has to give. Part of looking after our mental health is having clear boundaries around what we can carry and what we let go.

What are some things you can let go of? Where do you need to say, "No?" Who can you give some of the responsibility to?

We all have an inner critic, but we can train the critic to be quiet and strengthen our self-compassion. It is okay to analyse what we have done so we can learn, but we need to do this with kindness. It is important that we learn to really listen to our inner thoughts and challenge them when we need to. You could:

Journal Your Thoughts - Write everything down as you think it, unfiltered, then read over what you have written. How would you respond if your friend was saying those things about themselves? Are you using extreme words like always or never? How could you change these thoughts to be more helpful? e.g., "I screwed up again!" could be changed to, "I made a mistake, but it can be repaired. I'm better than I used to be."

Catch Your Thoughts - Too often thoughts happen without us really being conscious of them. If you are feeling down/angry/sad, there will be a thought behind it. As you think something about yourself, try to stop for a moment. Examine the thought, is it really true? Are you being too hard on yourself? But don't get stuck on a specific thought. They will come, but we also need to let them go. Just because you think something, doesn't make it true.

As parents, we can get so consumed and when our kids are little, we can even forget what it's like to have an adult conversation. Our brains need to keep learning and being stimulated. That doesn't mean attempting to do a PhD or doing something overly challenging, but it can help to add activities to keep your thinking sharp. You could:

- Read regularly. Try to have a book with you rather than your phone. That way when you have 10 minutes, you can read, rather than mindlessly scroll.
- Listen to audio books or podcasts. These are great because you can listen while driving, cleaning, etc.
- Puzzles, crosswords, sudoku, etc.
- Challenge yourself to learn a new skill. You can learn almost anything on YouTube now. You don't even have to start a class or be committed to meetings.

What will you try to add?

Emotional

Emotional self-care is a process in which we are aware of our emotions and we care for our emotional needs. Part of this is learning to stay in the moment, without being hijacked by overwhelming emotions. Another part is allowing ourselves to move through emotions. Having some calming strategies that you practise regularly can be helpful. If you practise them when you are already calm, it will be much easier to do them when you really need them. Here are some ideas:

Breathing - Controlled breathing is something you can do anywhere, at any time. If we can learn to be in tune with our body, it is easier to retain our calm before things get too out of control. Do a quick body scan. Are your muscles tight and your shoulders near your ears? Is your jaw clenched? Look for your warning signs and use them for your cues to breathe.

Affirmations or Mantras - Find affirmations/mantras that you can use when emotions are rising. Have it as a tool to help bring the clarity you need. Some you can try are: "I can do hard things," "I am enough," 'It's not personal, it's developmental," "This will pass." Find what works for you and use it often.

Also, caring for your emotional well-being is doing the things that you love. What lights you up? What are your passions? How can you make time for these? You may have to make some compromises, but you can still meet that need. For example, if you love painting, but it is hard to paint when you have children hanging off you, you could still find a way to be creative. You could draw or colour, 'paint' on the iPad (no mess and you don't have to worry about it drying out). Do what you can until there is time for it again.

Quick Relaxation Techniques

Relaxation doesn't have to take long, but it helps if it is done regularly. Try to find those small pockets of time, such as:

- Driving or riding in the car.
- While rocking your baby or toddler.
- Nursing a baby.
- Waiting for kids while in the car.
- Watching from the sidelines while kids play sports at a practice or a game.

Here are some quick ways to relax:

Just Breathe
- Breathe in slowly.
- Hold your breath when you have filled your lungs.
- Count 1 – 2 – 3 – 4 – 5 …keep holding 6 – 7.
- Now blow out all of the air slowly, until it's all gone.

A relaxation response takes 12 breaths (roughly 2 minutes). However, if you do deep breathing regularly, it can work after 6 breaths. So keep practising.

Quick Body Relax

1. Scrunch up your face then relax.
2. Raise your eyebrows a few times.
3. Drop your jaw, open and close your mouth.
4. Roll your shoulders.
5. Shake your hands and arms.
6. Take five slow breaths.
7. Repeat.

Do a Body Scan

Bring your attention to each of the following body parts one at a time:

1. Toes → ball of the foot.
2. Calves → quads.
3. Stomach.
4. Shoulders.
5. Neck.
6. Jaw.
7. Face.

As you work your way through them, try to consciously relax them and release the tension. It can help to tighten the muscles first and then release.

Parenting Mantra/Affirmations

Find the Mantra/Affirmation that works for you, not all of them will, and that's okay. Just have a couple that you can use when you need a reminder.

- This is not an emergency.
- I can handle this.
- I breathe in calm, I breathe out calm.
- My child is doing the best he/she can.
- Behaviour is an unmet need.
- Behaviour is communication.
- I'm safe.
- I have everything I need right now.
- Connection before correction.
- My child is not giving me a hard time, they are having a hard time.
- I will breathe and respond calmly in this moment.
- Parenting has ups and downs, I can ride the waves.
- I don't love these struggles but I love my kids.
- My child and I are learning as we go.
- I will choose to model what I want to see in my children.
- Even when it is hard, my kids and my family still love me.
- We all have bad days. This too shall pass.
- I am the best parent for my child.
- I am still a good parent, even when I lose my cool.
- Even though my kids come first, it doesn't mean I come last.
- I am enough for my child(ren), even when I don't feel like I am.
- I deserve to ask for help when I need it.
- Self-care is not a luxury.
- This is only a season.
- I can't control everything, but I can control how I react.
- Being present is more important than being perfect.
- It's okay to slow down and do less when I need to.
- I will make mistakes. What matters is how I learn and grow from them.
- What I messed up today, I can fix tomorrow.

(Some of these were inspired from https://www.happiestbaby.com/)

6.

Mindfulness

Mindfulness for Children

Mindfulness has always been an effective tool for self-regulation. However, more recently, it has become an on-trend buzzword. Mindfulness has been touted as a somewhat mysterious thing that people do to help solve their problems. The truth is that mindfulness is quite simple. Being mindful is as simple as intentionally bringing yourself into the present moment. It involves being aware of your senses, thoughts, and emotions in that moment, not letting your thoughts run away to the 'what ifs.'

While mindfulness is simple, its simplicity doesn't take away from how incredibly effective it is. The positive outcomes of practising mindfulness have been well-researched and go far beyond just feeling relaxed (Flook et al, 2010, Napoli, 2004). It has been found that teaching children mindfulness techniques from an early age significantly improves their performance academically, socially, and emotionally. This has led to many schools adopting mindfulness practices into their curriculum.

Children seem to thrive once they have been taught mindfulness. One reason for this is that it helps build the neurological pathways that promote focus and cognitive control. Research has found that practicing mindfulness increases the density of the part of the brain known for storing memories and helping with emotional control (hippocampus) (Hölzel et al, 2011). It was also found that there was a decrease in the grey matter in the amygdala. This is the centre for stress, fear, and anxiety, including our fight-or-flight response, meaning we become less reactive. Finally, the prefrontal cortex, where the brain makes decisions and controls behaviors, was found to become more activated leading to stronger executive functioning skills such as planning and problem-solving. By practising mindfulness at the critical stages of brain development in childhood, children build the pathways necessary for increased focus, control, and emotional regulation. Skills that will stay with them throughout their lives.

The Benefits of Mindfulness

1. Cognitive Benefits

Several studies (Flook et al, 2010; Napoli, 2004) have shown that implementing a school-based mindfulness program results in greater academic performance with

188

improved attention, ability to plan, and capacity to switch focus and remember details. By practising focus, children were able to improve their attention, which meant they performed better. Improved performance is always more likely when we can focus, whether it is in school, sports, work, or leisure pursuits. Mindfulness has even been shown to help children with Attention Deficit Hyperactivity Disorder become more focused (Zhang et al, 2017). Children with ADHD have greater difficulty with executive functioning and focus than neurotypical children. While mindfulness doesn't 'cure' ADHD, the fact that there is an improvement in executive functioning skills for these children shows how effective mindfulness can be.

2. Social Benefits

By practicing mindfulness, children become more aware of their feelings and, thus, less reactive when triggering situations arise. When we are less reactive, we can listen and communicate more effectively. Once children are aware of their own emotions, they gain the ability to understand these emotions in others and, therefore, have empathy for them. Some studies have even found that bullying dropped significantly after a mindfulness program was run in schools (Zhou et al, 2016). The assumption is that children who had bullied other children gained a better understanding of how they felt and could translate this to others. They became more empathetic and understanding of those around them. This shift makes a huge difference to the difficulties children face in the playground. School is such an incredibly social environment, with constant frustrations and misunderstandings. When children are aware of their feelings and develop empathy, they will naturally be able to interact with others more effectively.

3. Emotional Benefits

Children, like all of us, feel anxiety and stress but they don't always know how to manage these overwhelming emotions. Often, difficult emotions can come out as anger, restlessness, or even hyperactivity, when it is, in fact, the child internally struggling to handle those big feelings. Participating in mindfulness activities helps children manage their stress levels and improve their overall sense of well-being. Mindfulness can help slow our heart rate and breathing. This causes the fight/flight response to switch off and lowers the levels of the stress hormone (cortisol) in our bodies. And as I mentioned above, it also strengthens the thinking

189

area of our brain, while simultaneously shrinking the emotional area. This means that not only does mindfulness reduce your child's stress, it also makes their brains less reactive to stress in the long term.

There is no doubt that mindfulness can bring a sense of calm and help us manage stress. The ripple effect of this calm is amazing. When we feel calm, we can minimise anxiety, think clearly, and perform better. As a result, self-esteem and feelings of self-worth improve. Imagine the long-term impact of building self-worth in our children, especially to counteract the challenging adolescent years. Mindfulness also creates good habits for the future. Children will ultimately face challenges in life, but with a good grounding in mindfulness, they will have the skills to stop, calm themselves, and work through the situation without being reactive.

Mindfulness is a powerful tool to help our children develop awareness and focus. With research showing that mindfulness improves cognitive, social, and emotional functioning, we can be sure there will be positive flow-on effects for the child's well-being, attention, self-regulation, and social skills. Equipping them with these skills for life.

Mindfulness ABCs

Aware
What am I feeling?

Breathe
Slow your breathing

Choose
When calmer, choose
what you can do

@The_Therapist_Parent

Mindfulness Activities

To have a significant effect, mindfulness needs to be practised regularly. Making it a part of the daily routine for your family is particularly effective, as the best way to teach children about the concept is to model it yourself. Let them see you stop your activities, concentrate on your breath, and return to the situation in a noticeably calm state.

There are many fun mindfulness activities for kids, but it will always be best to do them with your children. Be careful to keep mindfulness activities a positive practice. Don't use them as a punishment or as a shaming tool. You will simply lose the benefits of the exercise by doing that.

The following are activities you can try with your children.

Focus On Senses: Ask children to stop and focus on their senses. What can they smell, see, hear, taste, and touch? You could get them to pretend to be a superhero with super-strong abilities. Or they could find three things for each sense (like Eye Spy for each sense), or any variation that encourages them to become more mindful of the world around them. Such activities allow us to practise focusing on the present moment while being aware of the information from our senses.

Glitter Jar: These are easy to make and very effective for focusing and holding attention. Get a plastic bottle. Fill about a quarter of it with warm water. Add some glitter glue and some extra glitter. You could also add a drop of food colouring to provide more interest. Then fill the rest with warm water and put the lid on.

Shake the jar and watch the glitter swirl around. Talk to your children about how our thoughts and feelings can be like the glitter – all mixed up. Then sit and watch the glitter slowly settle to the bottom. If you add some controlled breathing to the process, your child can use these techniques to calm themselves the whole time the glitter settles. Explain that, like the glitter in the jar, we can think clearer and feel better when our thoughts and feelings settle.

Mindful Walk: Walk with your child and take notice of all the things around you. Again, encourage them to notice what they can see, hear, smell, taste, and feel. Have them look for bugs, a particular plant they can identify, or choose a shape to spot. You could also look for pictures in the clouds.

Blow Bubbles: To blow bubbles, you need to use long, slow, calming breaths. You will pop everything before it forms properly if you blow too hard and fast. Have children focus on the bubbles as they grow and float away. You can also get them to imagine that the bubbles are their worries, and they can have fun popping them.

Pinwheel: Like blowing bubbles, you need to get the breath right to spin a pinwheel. Also, encourage children to focus on the colours as it spins. If you don't have a pinwheel, you can find free templates online to make your own.

Blowing up Balloons: Blowing up balloons can be a great way to do long slow breaths. You can also add that when children blow into the balloon they are blowing in all the worries or difficult feelings. Then they breathe in calm feelings. Have fun with it. You can let the balloon go and watch all thoughts/difficult feelings fly all over the room. Or you could tie it up and hit it and bounce it around, or even pop it. Whatever will work for your child.

Texture Game: Put different objects into a bag. Have your child use only their sense of touch to feel each thing and describe what they are like. Are they soft, hard, smooth, or rough?

Taste Test: Gather a range of small foods items (e.g., sultanas, nuts, etc.) Blindfold your child and have them put the food into their mouth but not eat it right away. Get them to fully taste each one. Guide them and ask a range of questions. Have them roll it around on their tongue and ask, "What does it feel like?" When they chew it, what is the texture? What is the main flavour? Ask if the taste changes the more they chew. Mindful eating is not just enjoyable, it is a strategy that can be applied throughout life. It helps you fully enjoy a meal and aids digestion as you are more likely to eat slowly and chew your food well.

Tummy Breathing (Boat or Toy): Have children lie down and place a paper boat or a toy on their tummies. Get them to take slow breaths while trying to fill their lungs. Have them watch the boat rise as they breathe in and fall as they breathe out, just like the waves of the ocean.

Blow Out the Candles: Not real candles, that would be a bit difficult and possibly dangerous. Have your child hold their hands up and pretend that their fingers are candles. Have them SLOWLY blow across them all, in one breath. They will want to do it fast but try to encourage them to do it slowly. Do it several times. This strategy is great for kids who like the sensation of the blowing on their hands, it can be very relaxing.

Muscle Relaxation (Robot/Rag Doll): Have children sit or lie down. Ask them to squeeze every muscle as tight as a robot. Have them hold this for a few seconds and then release it to be floppy like a rag doll. Ask them to describe how they feel after this. Repeat a few times.

Heartbeat Exercise: Have your child run or jump, anything that increases their heart rate. Then ask them to sit and close their eyes, placing their hand on their heart. Get them to breathe slowly and notice their heart rate slowing as their body calms. This encourages them to become more aware of their body and what happens inside them. This activity also teaches children to notice when their heart rate increases with anxiety or anger and allows them to understand how to calm it.

Guided Meditation: You will find many great meditations online. The Smiling Minds app has free guided meditations that are really helpful, with options specifically aimed at children in different age groups. My favourite is to imagine that I am at the beach. I allow my breath to become rhythmic like the waves, and feel the sun on my skin and sand beneath my feet. I can hear the birds and the waves, taste the salt in the air, and smell the ocean in the breeze. As you can see from this short example, these meditations don't have to be complicated and can be imagined if you don't want to use technology for the activity. Just find something that you and your child enjoy.

Finding Your 'Special Place' Activity

A great way for kids to learn to relax and feel calm is to find their 'special place.' This special place is somewhere they can imagine, where they are calm and happy. Using guided imagery in relaxation reduces anxiety and builds resilience, it reduces anxiety for several reasons;

1. Security: Having a special place in your mind means that you can create a safe place you can go to whenever you need it. You don't have to physically be there to experience the calm and peace that the special place brings.

2. Predictability: This special place is YOUR place, it only changes if you want it to. Using this technique often will mean that you can go to the same predictable environment. This is especially helpful when things are chaotic or routines have to change.

3. Having Some Control: You, and you alone, have the power to create this special place. Only you can decide what and who are there. This is particularly helpful at times when so many things are out of our control.

All of these are effective to reduce stress and build resilience. However when we combine them with controlled breathing and mindfulness, this becomes an incredibly powerful calming technique. If practised regularly, like anything, it will become easier and the ability to relax will happen more quickly. You will literally be able to train your brain to calm.

Finding Your Special Place

To find your special place, whether you are an adult or a child, start by closing your eyes. Think of a time you felt completely happy and relaxed. Where was it? Were you on holiday somewhere special, or was it a more 'everyday' location? Your special place could be a favourite tree, cubby house, anywhere that resonates with you. It is amazing how often water seems to be part of someone's special place. So often it is the beach, river, or pool. But it doesn't have to be, just anywhere that you have felt calm and happy.

When working with children, I find it best to have them draw their ideas. I usually start by tracing around their hand. Then when they have thought about their special place, have them draw this in the palm of the hand.

At each finger write See, Hear, Smell, Taste, and Touch.

Have them imagine their special place in detail. Go through the five senses and write them in the fingers. What can they see in that special place, what are the sounds around them, what does the air smell like, what can they taste, and what does it feel like on their skin.

By doing this, you are adding mindfulness to the relaxation. This engages the whole body in the relaxation and creates space for calm. They become aware of their body in the safe space and activate all areas of their brain in the imagery.

This in itself is a very powerful relaxation. However if you add some controlled breathing, it will be even more effective. Have them trace their hand with their finger. Tracing to the top of a finger, take a slow deep breath in.

Hold your breath at the top, and then slowly breathe out as you go down the finger. Adding arrows to the drawing will help them remember how to do this. I have also created a wooden puzzle of this activity with different 'special place' images you can use, it is on my website if you are interested.

Adding this routine to your day will be helpful to build the skill of relaxation. At night in bed is also a great place to practise. Chances are, children will fall asleep soon after they start. If you practise this regularly, it will be easy for your child to do when they are stressed or anxious and they need to calm. By doing this technique with their hand, they can easily remember the picture, the five senses and the breathing. They also know that they have this special technique to use wherever they are. They can use it anywhere and any time.

7.

Working Through

Anxiety

Anxiety and the Brain

The brain is amazing. We once thought that neural pathways were set and we could do nothing to change them. We now know that the brain is constantly changing. Every time we learn something, a new pathway is made. The more you practise a thought or action, the stronger those pathways are. That's why learning something can seem hard to begin with. Your brain has to make brand-new neural pathways. But as those memories and learning are practised, it becomes easier because the paths those thoughts or actions need to travel along now exist. The ability of our brains to change like this is called neuroplasticity.

When it comes to anxiety, neuroplasticity is both a blessing and a curse. When our brain perceives a threat, the pathways that control our subsequent actions take priority over other wiring in the brain. If we are anxious, our brains will automatically focus on the threat and what strategies we can use to deal with it. For example, when we are in the fight/flight (anxious) mode, and we have had a tantrum (fight) or have avoided a situation (flight) in the past, we will automatically want to use that strategy again. However, the good thing about neuroplasticity is that we can change this automatic response. It just takes practise.

The 'fight or flight' response is an autonomic response from the sympathetic nervous system. It is a good thing; we need it. When there really is danger, we need our bodies to react quickly and without too much thought so we can respond quickly. The problem is, when we are anxious, this response is essentially an overreaction, and we need to learn to calm it. There is another nervous system called the parasympathetic nervous system. This system is responsible for the 'rest and digest' responses, basically the opposite of anxiety. The primary nerve that controls this system is called the Vagus nerve. So why am I going into so much detail about the nervous systems? Well, when the Vagus nerve is stimulated, neuroplasticity is more effective.

Suppose an event of anxiousness has created a pathway that leads to a fight/flight response. If we can stimulate the Vagus Nerve through the use of new strategies, our brains will learn this new way of responding more easily. The key to stimulating the Vagus Nerve is to slow your diaphragmatic breathing.

This is why Psychologists go on and on about using controlled breathing as a strategy for relaxation. Quite literally, when we breathe slowly, a message is sent to the Vagus nerve which then causes the body to release calming chemicals.

So, I will say it again, find a way to teach your child controlled breathing. There are so many ways to do this, and they can be fun and imaginative. You can pretend to savour the smell of a cup of hot chocolate and then slowly blow on it to cool it down. Or get your child to focus on their breathing by placing their hand on their diaphragm (just below where their ribs meet in the middle) and focus on breathing in slowly. As they breathe in, get them to concentrate on making their tummy come out, not their chest. Then have them slowly breathe out. It doesn't matter which technique you use as long as the breathing is slow. It helps if you can practise this when your child is in a calm state, such as at bedtime. This way, when they recognise that they are anxious, being able to do the breathing will come more easily. They won't have to learn it in the midst of their anxiety.

Building Brave

Now that I have explained some ways to calm the nervous system during anxiety, how do we keep the momentum going and build courage in our children? We need our kids to see their bravery so that when anxiety arises, they know they have overcome it before. They need to understand that anxiety and fear are normal. We all feel these emotions. Even the bravest people in the world get anxious. Kids usually think that bravery is doing something without fear. Still, we need to teach them that bravery is actually doing something despite fear.

1. Lead by Example

In your children's eyes, you are their hero; well, for young children, at least. Most likely, your children assume you never get scared. Some parents think they have to uphold this image, but doing so might just be doing your children a disservice. I'm not saying you should tell your kids about every worry you have. We certainly don't need to put more stress or worry on them. But it is okay for them to know that you are a bit nervous about a big presentation you must do at work or about meeting people for the first time. Sharing such feelings normalises anxiety for our kids. It is particularly effective if you include them in the strategies that you use to manage your anxiety, such as, "I'm feeling a bit nervous about tomorrow, so I'm going to go for a walk to feel better." Or, "I need to do some breathing to feel more calm. Will you do it with me?"

2. Use Imagination

The imaginative world is so real to kids. It would be such a waste not to tap into it. Get creative with your child. What is something that they could use to feel brave? You could choose a rock together. You could both hold the rock and put brave feelings into it. That way (when they have to go to school or somewhere that triggers anxiety), they can have their rock in their pocket and feel the brave feelings. Another way might be to wear Superman underwear to remind them to be brave. It can seem completely ridiculous, but if it works for your child, go for it.

3. Celebrate Bravery, Not Success

Nothing reinforces fear more than failure. If a child is scared when they try and fail something, chances are they won't try again. Changing how failure is viewed can make a massive difference to how someone ultimately feels about an event. If a child was scared to try something new, but they did try it, then that is a success. Praise your child for the bravery to have a go and make sure you label it as 'brave.' Kids need to realise they are brave even if things don't work out the way they wanted them to. When they realise that they did have some success, they will be more likely to have the confidence to try again.

When we understand how to manage anxiety and build our kids' confidence to overcome it, we will build their bravery for future success.

One of the most precious gifts we can give
our child is holding space for them.
Stopping, listening and really seeing all that
they are

@The_Therapist_Parent

How Can I Help My Anxious Child?

Anxiety is real, whether you are a child or an adult. Adults can be quick to dismiss a child's anxiety as them being 'shy' or 'not confident,' but the truth is anxiety can feel crippling, even for children. Often, adults don't understand a child's worries, and therefore don't see them as important. But for the child, that worry can be overwhelmingly distressing.

Anxiety is rarely logical, but that doesn't make it any less real. We all have fears that don't make sense to others. Someone afraid of spiders can be absolutely terrified of a tiny, harmless spider, and we seem to accept this as okay. But a child's fear of the dark or going somewhere new, while often dismissed, is just as valid.

Telling your child, "Everything is okay, there is nothing to worry about" or, "Don't be silly," will not help them. They want to listen to you, they wish they could, but their brain won't let them. When we become anxious, our brain and body go into fight/flight/freeze mode. Quite literally, the logical thinking part of our brain switches off and the emotional part takes over. It is trying to keep us alive, so it exaggerates sounds, sights, and feelings to promote rapid breathing and give the body the oxygen boost it needs to take action. However, hyperventilation may result if our muscles do not immediately need this influx. That's why we jump at every sound when we are scared. We are ready to do what we need to in order to survive.

So, when we try to talk to our kids logically about why they don't need to be anxious, they simply can't hear us. In such situations, children also feel like you don't understand what they are going through, so they have difficulty believing your reasoning.

So, What Can We Do To Help?

Stop, Empathise, Calm, Problem-Solve, and Make a Plan

The most important thing you can do when your child is anxious is to 'stop' with your child. Don't race ahead and try to fix the situation. Don't give them lots of things to do or think about. Just stop. When we stop with our child, we put aside everything else and focus on them. Because of this, they feel as though you are with them; they aren't alone.

Empathise with your child. Even if you don't really understand why they are anxious, just connect with their feelings. We have all been anxious and can relate to a racing heart, shortness of breath, and the feeling that there might not be a light at the end of the tunnel. Connect with that feeling. You could say, "I know it is hard to feel worried." Let them know you do understand and appreciate that the situation is challenging.

The only way your child will be able to think logically again is to be **Calm**. When we are calm, the logical part of our brain can take over from the emotional part again. The best (and easiest) way to feel calm is to do slow, diaphragmatic breathing. When we breathe slowly, our body triggers the Vagus nerve, which causes our whole body to calm. Breathing slowly isn't just a distraction. It physically changes how our body works. There are many great ways to do breathing activities with children. See the *Breathe Together* section on page 50.

My favourite breathing technique is to have your child trace around their hand. This can be done with or without paper and a pencil. As they trace up the outside of a finger, ask them to breathe in. At the top of the finger, get them to hold their breath. Then have them breathe out as they go down the other side of their finger. Continuing this for each finger will help them slow their breathing - and they usually like the sensation of tracing their hand.

There are more **fun relaxation techniques** on page 184 and **mindfulness** activities on page 191.

When your child is calm, you can start **Problem-Solving**. It is essential to involve your child in this so they feel some control over the anxiety. This control will not be experienced if you are making decisions for them or just telling them what to do. Have your child come up with ideas. Even if they seem crazy, don't dismiss them. Talk them through. Ask, "What would happen if we did that?" Then they can work out which strategies to try.

Once you have come up with some ideas together, **Make A Plan** for how they can carry them out. They might want to try a few things to see if they work. You can also work together to create a stepped plan, breaking the worry down into smaller, more manageable steps. That way, whatever caused the anxiety might not seem so overwhelming.

Anxiety Isn't All Bad

When our kids are anxious, they often feel something is wrong with them. They believe others don't worry as much and can seem to do things easily. If your child feels that there is something wrong, then there is a high likelihood that they will worry about this too.

If we can explain what anxiety is, we can help our children feel that what is happening is normal. Everybody gets anxious, and it is something that our body is supposed to do. It can be helpful to explain that for early humans (cave men and women), it was essential to be ready to fight, run away, or freeze in order to protect themselves from dangerous animals or situations. This was how they stayed alive. Although it is unlikely that we will be attacked by a wild animal now, our bodies still respond in the same way. So, their body is doing exactly what it needs to do. The problem is that their brain is working a bit too hard to keep them safe.

Catch Unhelpful Thoughts.

Thoughts and worry have a cyclic relationship. When we have a thought that makes us worried, we then feel anxious, which triggers more thoughts, worries, and so on. But if we can catch the unhelpful thought before it spirals out of control, we can change it to something more helpful. Now remember, we can't think logically when we are anxious. Thinking logically is only something you can do when you are calm. As you teach your child what unhelpful thoughts are, they can learn to catch them before they spiral into worry. Explain that these thoughts are any that make them feel 'not good.' They could be feelings of sadness, anger, frustration, annoyance, etc.

Unhelpful thoughts usually have some common words, such as Always, Never, Not Fair, or Will. For example, "I always get that wrong!" "I never win anything." "I didn't get picked for the team. It's not fair!" "I will fail the test." These extreme words can evoke intense emotions.

While unhelpful thoughts may have an element of truth, they are never completely true. Once you have identified the exaggerated thought, work together to find the more helpful thought.

It is important to note that the helpful thought is not just the opposite of the unhelpful thought. If the unhelpful thought was, "He always takes my stuff," the helpful thought would not be, "He never takes my stuff," because that wouldn't be true either. In addition, the purpose of a helpful thought is not to make you feel wonderful. It is just supposed to make you feel a little bit better. When we can lift our mood a little, it makes the situation somewhat easier to handle. So, for this example, the helpful thought could be, "He sometimes takes my stuff," or "He usually asks first." Your child might still be a little upset about the situation, but not as badly as they were when using the extreme statement. Work together to pick the most helpful thought.

Unhelpful/Poisonous

- He (Always) takes my stuff
- He (Never) gets in trouble
- It's (Not) fair otherkids stay up late
- They (will) hurt me

Helpful/Antidote

- He usually asks first
- He sometimes gets in trouble
- Some kids go to bed earlier than me
- I haven't been hurt before, there are safe people

Learning to change our thoughts takes practise. It is unlikely to work instantly, but eventually, children will start to recognise they are using extreme words in their thinking and be able to adjust accordingly. Have them practise changing extreme words when they are calm; eventually, it will happen automatically.

Anxiety is hard for both children and adults, but there are things we can do to help. When we recognise that our child is struggling and join with them to bring a sense of calm, we build the connection that they need to learn the strategies necessary to manage it.

It is important to teach your child how to calm themselves, problem-solve, and catch unhelpful thoughts. Still, the essential factor is that they feel you understand and are with them every step of the way.

We don't have to understand our child's anxiety but we do need to help them to feel heard.

@The_Therapist_Parent

Managing Anxiety

When children are anxious, it doesn't always look how we think it should. You may find that your kids fight more, are reluctant to complete tasks, are more aggressive, or just seem to act out of character. It is not uncommon for anxiety to show itself through anger, which is why it can be easily missed. So, how do we manage anxiety and encourage our kids through this experience?

1. Acknowledge It

We can't manage what we don't recognise. Ask your child how they feel about what is going on in their world. Ask them to explain how they feel about going to school, what's happening with their friends, on sporting teams, or whatever they are involved with. If they are young, or find it difficult to express their emotions, then name the experiences for them. You could say, "It seems like something is going on for you at the moment. Is there anything you are worried about? It's okay to feel nervous about..."

Be careful not to jump on their worries with answers. Anxiety is rarely logical, so saying what worries them is 'silly' or not really an issue is not helpful. It is real to them. Acknowledge that their fears would make them feel scared. Now, you do not need to agree with the fear; just validate the emotion. You could say, "Yes, that does sound scary" or, "I understand why you feel worried." When a child feels heard it helps them feel safe enough to work with you to find a solution.

2. Explain Anxiety

It doesn't really matter how old your child is, explaining the basics of anxiety helps them understand what their body is doing. Such an explanation provides the child with the opportunity to realise that their feelings are normal.

You don't need to go into the brain science of anxiety with your child, but you might be surprised by how much they are able to understand. Explain that it is our brain's job to keep us safe from anything harmful. But, sometimes, our brain works too well and causes us to feel anxious when we are actually safe (see *Anxiety and the Brain* on page 197 for more information.)

To help children understand the concept, you can pose a question for them to consider: "Back when there were cavemen, if a Sabre-tooth Tiger came into your cave, what would you have to do?" The answers usually involve a fight-or-flight response. From there, you can explain what happens to the body in these situations. A fast heartbeat, quickened breathing, or muscles that feel tight or wobbly suggest your body thinks it needs to react with a fight or through flight. But as there are no Sabre-tooth tigers now, we need to recognise when our bodies begin to have these reactions, and rather than responding with a tantrum (fight) or resistance/defiance (flight), we train ourselves to be calm so that we can think clearer and feel better.

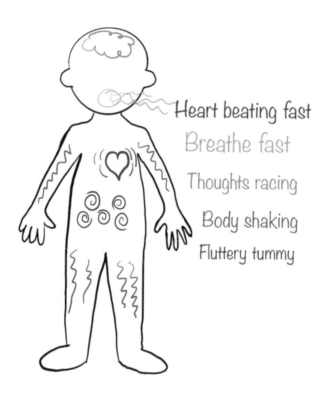

Heart beating fast
Breathe fast
Thoughts racing
Body shaking
Fluttery tummy

You can also have children draw these feelings and where they occur in their bodies. This visual representation helps describe what happens in situations that make them anxious and provides them with an understanding that these feelings are normal. When they learn what their body tells them, they can connect the physical reaction to the emotion. And when we give them skills to calm themselves, the physical changes become a warning that they need to use their tools to calm.

3. Release the Anxiety

Before we can do any problem-solving or any logical thinking, we need our kids to calm their bodies. Quite literally, when someone is anxious, the logical part of the brain shuts down. That's why we can be highly anxious about things that make no logical sense. There is no point in telling your child everything is safe and they don't have to worry. They are worried, and while they are in a state of 'fight' or 'flight' they will not respond to your reasoning. Try the *Mindfulness Activities* on page 191 to help them calm.

4. Make a Plan

We can only begin to talk about problem-solving once we have done each of the previous steps. Once the child feels heard, understands what they are experiencing, and can calm themselves, they can logically cope with the worries they have. If we try to skip the previous steps, we will likely hit resistance and not assist our kids in finding peace.

Talk about what, specifically, worries them. What are some things they feel will help? What else could they do? Work together to come up with ideas.

They could be worried about friendships and playing with other kids. Role-playing works well with children in these situations. You could have them practise asking someone else to play or explore options for different outcomes when playing games (e.g., what could you do if you lose? How might you react if you win? How could you encourage others? etc.)

When we help children understand why we all struggle with anxiety at times, and it is a natural way that our body tries to protect us, it becomes less scary. As we take them through what anxiety is, and validate it, they start to see that they have some control over it. When we can work with them and have a plan to manage these difficult situations, with practise, they will be able to progress through the anxiety.

208

All these feel like huge alarms going off in an under developed brain. The more we support them through, the more they learn that the alarm doesn't have to mean a threat

@The_Therapist_Parent

Managing Anxiety Activities

Brave Board

It is easy to forget the times we were brave or not even realise that what we experienced was bravery. But if we want our kids to build confidence and manage their anxiety, then we need them to recognise their strengths. If they can see all the times that they have been brave, then this is evidence that they can overcome fear and be brave again. Make a poster and decorate it however you like. Have your child brainstorm all the times they have been brave; chances are, you will need to help them remember these times. Once they have done something, they may forget how anxious they were to begin with. Locate this board where they can see it daily and remind them of all the challenges they have overcome. Add to the board when you can, as they do more and more brave things. That way, they can see that their bravery grows as they continue to overcome their anxiety.

Make a Coping Skills Toolbox

A Coping Skills Toolbox is a kit you create to help your child calm when they are upset, anxious, or worried. Talk to your child about what could help them calm when things are difficult. You could just use a shoe box or something similar, and put in activities and reminders that help your child calm. It could be blowing bubbles, play dough, breathing reminders, photos of their 'special place' or whatever works for them. When your child experiences anxiety, they can pick out an item from their Coping Skills Toolbox and put it to use.

Have Visual Reminders

When you're stressed and anxious, it's harder to read and take in information. Using visuals is a powerful way to help kids; when they are overwhelmed, it can be hard for them to figure out what to do.

You can make your own cards or posters to have as reminders. Work out with your child which breathing or mindfulness activity works best for them. Then draw or print out pictures that remind them how to do these. Have the visuals up where they can see them, or have small cards that you can laminate and take with you so you can have them when you are out. Practising these techniques regularly, even when kids aren't anxious, will make it easier when they are.

When in the midst of <u>anxiety</u> it can be hard to remember the times we were brave

Creating a brave board can help children have the evidence they need to see they are <u>brave</u>

@The_Therapist_Parent

Supporting Kids Through Separation Anxiety

Separation anxiety is a common form of anxiety in children. It can be quite difficult for both parents and children to manage. Little is worse than having your child cling to you desperately as you try to leave them. Separation anxiety is fuelled when a child experiences a new environment or new people but doesn't understand why their parent has to go without them. All of these are normal reasons to be anxious, but we can help them with the transition and their feelings of safety.

Anxiety exists for a reason: to protect us from threats. Our brain registers a threat and will try to protect us by sending us into a fight/flight/freeze response. If anxiety is intense, it will be triggered every time we are in a similar situation. The brain will literally look for similarities to a time when they were distressed and respond quickly so that same situation can be avoided. In the case of a child, it can be provoked every time their parent leaves, resulting in separation anxiety.

If your child is distressed, it is not the time to try to reason with them. There is no capacity for logical thinking in a state of anxiety (e.g., the fight/flight/freeze mode). The brain is focused on survival and nothing else. This is why some children seem to have superhuman strength as they grip on to you for dear life. They can't hear you say, "You will have fun. Your friends are here. You like your teacher." All they know is that their safe person is leaving. And they can't let that happen.

To overcome separation anxiety, we need to change the trigger response in the brain. This can't happen instantly. Just like learning anything, we need to do it over and over before we become proficient. In terms of separation anxiety, when children are triggered, they need to go through the emotion until there is calm again. Hence, the brain no longer registers this situation as a threat. If, when a child is triggered, you just leave them in the distressing environment, the brain makes a pathway that says, parent is leaving; display distress; parent won't go; I can stay safe. In an attempt to help, we often make their anxiety worse.

So how do we help? **Calm, Validate, and Problem-Solve.**

212

The first thing we need to do when our child experiences separation anxiety is help them calm. If they are distressed, their brain can't think and definitely can't learn. As a parent, you know what works to help your child. It might be a hug or letting them sit away from everyone else that allows them to feel calm again. The most important thing they need is a calm adult to be with them. We know that nervous systems will 'mirror' those around them, literally matching the arousal level of others. This is why it is vital that we remain calm in the face of their reaction. You could try doing some controlled breathing with your child. If they don't want to do it, you do it anyway, as it will still help.

Validating your child's feelings is also important in managing separation anxiety. If we try to talk our children out of their feelings, they generally think that we don't understand, and the anxiety will 'fight' more to be heard. However, if we acknowledge it, saying things such as, "I get it. It can be scary to leave mum." They feel understood and that you are on their side. This will also help to calm the brain, as the child begins to understand that they don't have to 'fight' alone. You don't have to agree with your child, but you do have to try to acknowledge their feelings.

Once they are calm and feel supported, they will have more capacity to problem-solve with you. It is essential to have them involved in this process. Together, work out what they can do to cope with the separation. It definitely helps to have some plans in place ahead of time. Talk to them at home when they are calm, and help them determine things they can do when they feel anxious about you leaving.

Most importantly, remember that getting through separation anxiety is a process. There is no instant cure. Just remember to help your child **Calm, Validate** their emotions, and **Problem-Solve** together. This reduces the triggered response, and they will eventually come through their anxiety. Ensure they are involved in every part of the process, as nobody will change if they have change forced on them. Children need to feel that they have some control and that you are there to support and guide them through their challenges.

When helping your child through separation anxiety

1. Calm: You know your child best and what they need to calm. There is no point trying anything until they are calm

2. Validate: They need to know you understand and are on their side

3. Problem Solve: Once they are ready you can make plan together

@The_Therapist_Parent

Ideas for Managing Separation Anxiety

1. Give Your Child Something of Yours

A parent can give their child something personally significant. It might be a necklace, a scarf, or a special rock or crystal. It could be anything that the child knows is important to you. Let the child use it only while you are apart, then when you return, they have to give it back to you. The child knows that the item is important and you will return for it. Now, some parents are upset by this because obviously, the child is more precious than the object, so surely the child knows that you will come back for them rather than just that thing. But that's not really what it is about. The item is simply a visual reminder that you will return. By giving them something special, you are also showing that you trust them and that they are mature enough to take care of it. This, in itself, helps to build confidence.

2. Keep a Picture of a Fun Time

Having a special location to imagine is a valuable relaxation technique. However, when a child is young or experiencing anxiety, it can be hard to focus on such a place in their imagination. Before the separation, talk to your child about their favourite place or holiday. Find a photo or something that reminds them of that place.

Use the photo or object to practise relaxation regularly at home. Talk to them about what it was like, what they enjoyed. Talk to them about what it looked like, what they could hear and smell. If it was the ocean, have them remember the sounds of the waves. Ask if they could remember the salty smell of the air or whether they had any memorable tastes. By doing this, you are connecting them with a happy, relaxing memory. When we connect with enjoyable memories, our bodies naturally relax.

If appropriate, you can have your child take the photo with them. When anxious or worried, they can look at the picture and connect with that calm emotion again. Now, I'm not saying that you can turn up to preschool/school and just pull out the photo when you leave, and all will be okay. Your child will likely still be

215

anxious; they may still be distressed. But if you do this ahead of time and involve them in the process, then they can use this strategy as a part of their plan to return to a state of calm. By doing this, you acknowledge that you understand they are anxious and show you know it is difficult for them. You also demonstrate that together, you can make it work.

3. Have a Step Plan

If you know your child has trouble separating from you, start small. But PLEASE involve your child in the process. You need them to feel some control over this process. Talk to them about different situations where they separate from you and discuss how scared they might feel. You could have them weigh up scenarios you know might cause anxiety, e.g., "Which is scarier, staying home with the other parent or staying at Grandma's?" "What about being at Grandma's during the day or in the evening?" Start by practising their least scary option, then talk to them about what helped and what was challenging. Tell them how proud you are of them for trying, and make a plan for next time. Make sure you are moving with the strategy too. Don't drop your child off then hang around until the very last minute. If you don't move with the plan as well, your child will be stuck in this stage of anxiety.

4. Social Stories

Social stories can help a child understand what they can expect to happen in certain situations. They can be fun to make, and doing this with your child can help you see the experience from their perspective while also giving them a sense of control.

Social stories are pretty simple to write. Start by saying where they are going. For example, "On Mondays, I go to preschool." Then write something about the preschool and, perhaps, their teacher. Write that Mum/Dad will have to leave, but that is okay because they always come back. Write about what happens during the day at preschool, using their usual routine. Don't try to rush it. Do it with as much detail as your child needs. Make sure you acknowledge how they feel by including these aspects too. For example, you might write, "Sometimes I feel sad when Mummy leaves." Then add what they can do if they feel this way.

216

If I feel sad, I can..." Finish the story by saying, "At the end of the day, I will be picked up by Mum/Dad." Have your child draw pictures to accompany these events or choose photos to use as a part of the story to give them a sense of ownership of the book.

5. Rituals

Routines and rituals give a sense of security and safety. Having a specific ritual, particularly around saying goodbye, will help your child know what to expect. This can relieve some of their anxiety. Ideas include having a special handshake, kissing each hand, or saying a specific phrase such as, "See you later, alligator." It doesn't matter what the ritual is; it is the predictability that is important.

Supporting a Child through 'Shyness'

The tendency to be shy can be a personality trait. These kids (and adults) tend to be cautious but thoughtful. They may warm up to people slowly, and they make strong friendship bonds once they do. We might be concerned for children with these traits because when they lack the confidence to join in, they can become distressed and avoid social or new experiences, often perpetuating a cycle of poor self-esteem.

How to Support a Child through Shyness

1. Talk about Feelings

All feelings are important. We honour who our child is, their level of social comfort, and their intuition, by saying things like, "I know it is hard when we meet new people. We can wait until you are ready. Your body will know when it is the right time." This tends to work better than saying, "You don't need to be shy. There is nothing to be afraid of," which will most certainly invalidate their experience and cause them to question their intuition.

2. Make a Plan

Kids who tend to be shy generally won't like new things sprung on them. They need time to plan and process what will happen in certain situations. Talk to your child ahead of time about where they are going, who will be there, what they will do, and roughly how long it will take.

3. Practise

A part of shyness is that kids don't know what to do or lack the confidence to do what is expected. You can role-play different social scenarios, such as asking another child to play, raising their hand to ask a question in class, looking at people in different situations, and holding their heads up. This will prime their brain for when they need to do these things, and as you connect with their feelings, they will feel safer knowing you are a secure base from which they can learn.

Have fun with this and encourage your child's effort. Be specific, saying things like, "I loved how clear your voice was." That way, they will know what aspects work, and every time they practise, they build confidence. When they do go to an event, and their first instinct is to stand back, you can say, "Remember what we practised? You can do this. I believe in you."

4. Find Kind People

When a child is overwhelmed, their brain is hypervigilant, looking for danger. It is the brain's job to look for danger so it can keep us safe. As the parent, we can be the calm influence that enables our child see that there is kindness around them. When someone says, "Hello" and smiles, point it out as something nice. If a child shares or asks them to play, then acknowledge that there are people around them who are safe and helpful. These quiet kids are good at observing. If we help them see the kindness around them, they will likely feel less fearful about joining in.

5. Social Stories

Social stories help children understand what they can expect in different situations. They can be fun to make and give your child a sense of control over their situation and behaviour. Use the instructions in *Ideas for Managing Separation Anxiety* on page 215 to help your shy child create their own social storybooks.

Children who feel shy are beautifully-natured, sensitive, and caring. We want to honour who they are while gently supporting them to explore and expand their comfort level in unfamiliar social situations. We don't have to turn them into raging extroverts, but by helping them recognize their feelings, have a plan, practise, and see the kindness in others, we provide them with the tools they need to have positive experiences.

Raising a Sensitive Soul

Do you have a child that people call a 'sensitive soul?' Or worse, are they labelled weak, a sook, or a wimp? Our culture has presented these children in a negative light, as if feeling deeply is a negative attribute. When we try to 'toughen kids up,' we are actually damaging a character trait. These children see, feel, and understand things that many people don't. If we nurture and guide these children so they can better understand and develop their sensitive side, they will have the potential to be incredible adults.

Sensitive kids aren't weak. They are actually far more aware of what is happening around them than most. They notice changes in their environment, seem to notice the moods of others more quickly, and tend to run through every possible scenario in their heads before making a decision. Yes, these children are more prone to anxiety, but their sensitive nature doesn't have to be a negative trait. They just need help to develop it.

It Starts at Home

Being in a highly social environment, such as school, can be exhausting for sensitive kids. The environment is noisy and unpredictable and they are surrounded by people whose moods are constantly changing. They need their home to be a safe place, somewhere calm that allows them to be themselves, wholly and completely. Relationships in families won't always be peaceful; that's an unrealistic expectation. But our kids need to know that no matter what, they are accepted for who they are, and nothing they do can change that. These children need constant connection so as not to feel alone. However, parents can think the bond they have with their child from birth will never change. And this simply isn't true. Connection is something you must work on. It can be broken, but it can also be restored.

Connection doesn't have to be expressed with grand gestures. The secure feeling of being connected with people who care about you comes from many little things throughout the day. Here are some ideas you can use to keep this bond with your child strong:

220

1. Play: This is such a powerful way to connect with children, especially if we enter their world and do not just play on our terms. When we let children choose the play, we tell them that they are important and that we like being with them.

2. Conversations: Have regular 'check-ins' and times that everyone is free to talk. The dinner table is a common place for the family to talk about their day, use the time or activity that works best for your family. It is easy to get caught up in endless errands and after-school activities, to the point you are left feeling like you're just surviving. It's not uncommon for parents to get their kids to bed at night and realise they didn't have a full conversation with their child that day. Sensitive kids need someone to confide in; they carry a lot of burdens. They need to know that there is a time they can talk to you.

3. Touch: Touch is a physical manifestation of connection. It doesn't have to be long hugs or back rubs, it can be as simple as touching your child's shoulder or tussling their hair. When we touch, we are in another's personal space, which creates intimacy. However, you can't force touch. If a child doesn't want you to hug, tickle, or touch them and you do so anyway, this will damage the connection.

4. Celebrate Strengths: Sensitive kids notice everything and take everything to heart. Where other kids may be able to let passing comments go, a sensitive kid may feel wounded. As this can be overwhelming, their strengths can be hard for them to see. We have to point out what their strengths are. Be careful not to make general comments like, "You are kind, caring, and smart." They probably won't believe you, but think that because you are their parent, you have to say that. Instead, point out when you see them exhibiting a strength. For example, "That was such a kind thing to do. Thank you." If we do this, we give them proof that they have these strengths.

5. Connection through Correction: We must be very careful when correcting sensitive kid's behaviour. A harsh word or tone is likely to cut them deeply. But we still need to correct them, all kids need guidance. However, disciplining (teaching) them is an opportunity to talk to them about what they did and why. Talk to your sensitive child about how their actions affected others, and then problem-solve. Work with them to determine what they can do to fix the problem.

Managing Emotions

Regulating emotions is difficult for any child as their brain is still developing. They can't always access the rational part of the brain needed to manage the complex situations of daily life. This is especially true for sensitive kids. They seem to feel so deeply that they are very easily overwhelmed and in emotional turmoil. That's why it is especially important these kids learn to recognise emotions and how to ride emotional waves without getting completely engulfed by them.

1. Recognising Emotions: The first step to limiting reactions to situations we can't control is to recognise our emotions. When our feelings are overwhelming, we go into autopilot, and our body/emotional brain takes over our decision-making. If we can stop and label the feeling, it is more likely we can find a solution and not feel out of control. You may have to coach your child on how to do this. For example, you could say, "It looks like you are feeling sad." But be open to them correcting you, as they might feel something completely different. The important thing is that they can recognise the feeling. You can read more about recognising emotions on page 242.

2. Relaxation: As anxiety is commonly associated with sensitive kids, it is really important that they learn relaxation and mindfulness. Their bodies tend to be in a constant state of stress, and they need to learn how to relax. Controlled breathing is a key to relaxation. When we learn to slow our breathing, it quite literally changes our body's chemistry and causes feelings of calm.

3. Boundaries: Sensitive kids often try to please everyone and simply don't recognise their own needs. We must teach them that it isn't their job to make everyone else happy. It is okay to help a friend, but they don't have to do everything the friend wants. This is something that takes practise and will not come naturally to them. You might have to role-play saying, "No" to others, or practise being assertive. It can help a sensitive child to have a script for what to say when someone crosses their boundaries and to practise holding their boundaries with a trusted adult in a non-confronting environment.

Sensitive kids have an amazing interpretation of the world. They aren't weak; in

222

fact, quite the opposite is true. It takes strength to experience the depth of feeling that they do. If we are to develop this as a positive attribute, we need to guide sensitive kids and not allow them to be damaged by the 'tough love' world around them.

Worry Bags Activity

Anxiety is a horrible thing. It is all-consuming. It takes over your body and mind and stops you doing what you want. Many people think kids don't get anxiety. "What have kids got to worry about?" The answer is, plenty.

Being a kid can be pretty stressful. You have to negotiate the social pressures from other kids in the playground, try to concentrate and sit still in class, as well as deal with siblings and the pressures of home. But on top of this, kids with anxiety also take on everyone else's worries. They will worry about things that adults believe are ridiculous. But the concern is genuine for the child. I have worked with children who feared their mother would be struck by lightning, that their parent's work would be robbed, and that a sinkhole would appear in their backyard. All these things sound pretty irrational, but that's just the thing, anxiety isn't rational.

How To Deal with Anxiety

When a child has anxiety, their worries can seem overwhelming. The best way to deal with this situation is to approach it one concern at a time. A mountain of fears can be reduced if we examine each one and decide what to do with it. Usually, children's worries can be divided into groups connected to significant people in the child's life.

1.Write Down the Worries

Write down as many worries as you can think of on a blank piece of paper. Leave space around each one so they can be cut out later. The concerns can be significant, small, or things that sound entirely outrageous. It doesn't matter. If the child has been worrying about it, write it down. Writing down a child's concerns serves two purposes. One, you can see exactly what the child worries about, and two, sometimes just writing down a worry helps the child externalise it and know that it isn't something they need to worry about.

2.Make Some Worry Bags.

Make a small bag for each person your child has concerns about. You can be as creative as you like. Use beautiful drawstring bags, paper bags, or just envelopes. It really doesn't matter. As long as you have a bag for each person the worries belong to (e.g., one for mum, dad, each sibling, class teacher etc.). I have even made a bag for God (or the universe) because really, sinkholes, cyclones, and floods are His worries.

3. Cut Out the Worries

Once you have your worry bags ready, cut out all the concerns and talk about who's bag each one should go into.

4.Put Each Worry in the Appropriate Bag.

Sometimes, you will need to talk through this process as children can become attached to these worries as their own. For example, let's take the 'Mum might not pick me up from school' worry. Your child might want to keep this worry because they believe it is actually about them. However, discuss that because mum is the parent, it is her job to pick you up. If she can't, then her job is to organise an alternative. It is not the child's worry.

5. Now, Have a Look in the Child's Bag.

There are usually only a small number of worries left for the child. This makes the concerns a lot more manageable. You can then engage the child in problem-solving to determine what they could do to alleviate their fears. Remind the child that they will have to keep putting concerns in other people's bags as they come up because worries do like to sneak back into your bag.

I have found this technique to be very effective, and it is something you can easily do at home whenever your child feels as though their worries are building up.

Worry bags.

Worries can be overwhelming. It can help to share them around

@The_Therapist_Parent

Relaxation Pillow Activity

When we are anxious, sleep is one of the first things to be impacted. Children are no different. When your child comes out of bed for the third glass of water, has a stomach ache, or seems to ask you deep philosophical questions, chances are they are anxious or worried about something. Regression and sleeplessness is a normal response to stress. It makes sense that at the times they feel unsafe, children would want to be with the people that make them feel safest. This means you may have a child kicking you in the middle of the night, after they have snuck in under your blankets.

Often, bedtime is difficult because there is nothing to distract children from their thoughts and they are left with all the worries of the day. Sometimes they don't even know what they are anxious about, just that they can't sleep. If they can get to sleep, they can be bombarded with nightmares.

They may not have had nightmares for years but all of a sudden, they seem to be having them every night. This is just another way for them to try and process the stress that they are under. There are lots of things that help with sleep. Having a regular bedtime, no screens for an hour before bed, being able to talk about worries during the day, and having a bedtime routine. Adding some relaxation to a bedtime routine will help to calm their bodies and minds so they can be in a space for restful sleep.

Relaxation Pillowcase

Even if you have done some sort of relaxation with your child before, when they really need to use it, they can forget. That's why having their relaxation reminders with them when they are in bed can be helpful.

Start with a plain pillowcase, any light colour is fine. You will need fabric markers. Make sure you put thick paper or cardboard in the pillowcase so that the markers don't bleed through.

Trace their hand on the pillowcase. Ideally you should do the hand that will rest on the pillow when they are sleeping. This is a good reminder of their controlled finger breathing. When they are in bed they can use their finger to trace around their hand. As they go up the finger they breathe in slowly, hold their breath at the top and then breathe out slowly as they trace down their finger.

Draw all over the pillowcase with all the things that make your child feel happy and safe. You can draw the 'special place' that they have as a relaxing memory. Draw anything that makes them smile. Talk through their five senses. What smells do they love, what feelings, what colours, what tastes, or sounds come from their special place?

You can target specific challenges. What are the worries or thoughts that they often have at bedtime. Do they feel alone or unsafe? What reminders could you add that will help them remember that they are okay? Write positive self-talk that they could say to themselves. If your child has been having nightmares, what would they like to dream about? Have them draw the dreams they want. It is especially helpful to draw an alternative ending to the nightmare they have had.

If they dreamt about snakes, could they turn them into lolly snakes and eat them. If they dreamt about monsters, could they shrink them and blow them away? The funnier the better, when it comes to changing dreams.

Some other ideas:

- Older children might like to add some inspirational quotes or affirmations.
- Have them draw all the people who love them and make them feel safe.
- What songs make them feel happy? Are there songs that make them smile or remind them of a great memory?

Every night they will now be able to add relaxation to their bedtime routine. These are all helpful reminders that they are safe and loved. At bedtime, slowly trace around their fingers. Slowly breathe in as you go up the finger, hold the breath at the top, and slowly breathe out as you go down the finger. Have your child practise doing this themselves. Reassure them that if they wake during the night, that they can do their breathing and remember the drawings on their pillow.

Of course, this doesn't mean that you have to kick them out of your bed if they come in. This will not last forever. Usually as the stress passes, so will the broken sleep. However, helping your child to relax before they go to bed will increase the chances of deep, relaxed sleep for everyone.

8.

Developing

Self-Esteem

How to Build Your Kid's Self-Esteem

One of the most common issues among children is poor self-esteem. We all have times when we feel bad about ourselves. But kids are trying to find their identity. They are learning what they are good at and what they aren't. They are working out how they are the same and different from others, and this is important. Self-esteem develops throughout our lives, but it is particularly important during childhood. In the early years, we gather information about ourselves and draw conclusions about our worth. These beliefs can stick with us into adulthood.

When We Talk about Self-Esteem, What Do We Really Mean?

Self-esteem refers to how good you feel about yourself. You don't have to like everything, but having good self-esteem means that you recognise that you have value. It can be defined by how much you appreciate and like yourself, even when things don't work out or you haven't done well. Your self-esteem is made up of the following:

- Self-confidence.
- Feelings of security.
- Identity.
- Sense of belonging.
- Feelings of competence.

When we break it down into these points, it is no wonder kids struggle with self-esteem. They have yet to have the life experience to develop any of these. They are learning everything, including where they fit in.

Why Self-Esteem Is Important

Kids who feel good about themselves have the confidence to try new things. They are not overly afraid of making mistakes. They can be proud of their efforts as they don't hold their worth in their achievements. When they aren't overly focused on the outcome, they are more likely to try their best. As a result, self-esteem helps kids do better at school, at home, and with friends.

Kids with low self-esteem often feel unsure of themselves. They don't try to join in or make friends because they think others won't accept them (they don't accept themselves, so why would others?) They may be susceptible to bullying and be less likely to stand up for themselves. They may give up easily or not try at all. Kids with low self-esteem find it hard to cope when they make a mistake, lose, or fail. They hold their worth in their achievements rather than in who they are as a person. As a result, they may not do as well as they could. It is a vicious cycle that can be difficult to break.

How Can We Help Build Children's Self-Esteem?

Connection with someone who you know loves you unconditionally, despite every failure, is the foundation for a healthy self-esteem. If a friend rejects them, they need to know that they are still loved and valued for who they are. Look for moments to surround your child with loving interactions. Pockets of time where you share a hug, touch, or show your appreciation. Spending time (even 15 minutes) of child-centred interaction, will fill their bucket and help them to feel seen and valued. Over time, when a child consistently feels loved, they will internalise this to become self-love (Lapointe, 2019.)

Focus Praise on the Effort

Often, parents, with the best of intentions, will flood their child with praise, thinking that this will build their self-esteem. If you tell them how great they are, they will feel good about themselves, right? Not necessarily. In fact, too much general praise, like, "Good job" or, "You're so clever," can actually have a negative impact. For a more detailed look at this concept and the behaviour it can manifest in our children, be sure to read *Is Praise Bad?* on page 107.

When we praise our kids, we must make sure that we are honouring the effort it took to achieve, not just the achievement. You can say, "I noticed you tried to sound out those words and didn't give up." Or, "Wow, you worked hard on that." Rather than, "You are such a good reader." When we focus on the attempt, our children feel they have made progress. This builds their self-esteem because they experience applying the effort and having it work toward a desired outcome. Kids will see that with effort comes improvement, making them more motivated to do things for themselves.

Step Back

Of course, as children are learning, they need our help. We have to be a role model and guide them. But don't be too quick to swoop in and do everything for them if you notice they are challenged. Children build self-esteem by being able to master things for themselves. Given the opportunity, they will see that even with mistakes, they can still achieve. When we take over all the time, we prevent them from developing their sense of independence. This goes for problem-solving too. Don't always jump in and tell kids what they need to do or how to 'fix' things. Ask them, "What do you think?" They may not know and will need you to provide feedback, but the more we have them practise, the more confident they will become in their own abilities.

Help Them Find Their Strengths

Everyone has strengths, but we don't always realise what they are. Our kids may have strengths that are different from ours. They may even be things that drive us crazy. Still, once we find their strengths, we need to build on them. Your child may have excellent attention to detail, which means that they are slow or have to get things 'just right' before they are satisfied. Although this can be frustrating at times, it is most definitely a strength in different circumstances, for instance, when they are building with Lego, coding, technical drawing, or any number of things requiring precision and attention to detail.

While kids are trying to figure out who they are, they may have any number of new interests. It is essential to let them try different things until they find 'their thing.'

An activity that can help kids identify their strengths and get a solid foundation of who they are is called the Tree of Me (which you'll find in the next section). This is a fun activity that helps kids see who loves and supports them, and their character traits and strengths.

Friendships

As children grow older, friendships become increasingly important. Having people outside your family who love and accept you for who you are is vital for healthy self-esteem. We don't always like who our kids become friends with, but as long as they are positive relationships for our children, then we need to support them. When we find friends, we find our tribe – people who 'get' us.

Friends should be encouraging and supportive. If friendships aren't building self-esteem though, they can be damaging, and this can be hard for kids to see. If this happens with your child, an activity called the Self-Esteem Bucket (which you'll find in the next section) provides an objective visual representation of the situation. This activity helps kids see what builds their self-esteem and what takes from it. By doing this, they can see what might not be working in their friendships and can then work with you to problem-solve the actions they could take.

While some kids are naturally more positive, self-esteem is something that develops in everyone. It is crucial that, as parents, we see that we can influence how our children's self-esteem develops. Self-esteem isn't all about hearing praise. It is having a sense of worth in who you are and the security of believing you are capable, no matter what. As parents, we can direct and guide our children to see this worth and develop their own confidence in their abilities.

Not everyone will like you and that's okay

@The_Therapist_Parent

Self-Esteem Bucket Activity

As discussed in *How to Build Your Kid's Self-Esteem* on page 229, developing a healthy self-esteem is incredibly important in all aspects of life. Self-esteem doesn't just happen, it grows and develops through experience. As parents, we can be intentional in building a healthy self-esteem in our children.

A great strategy that can be used to help kids build their self-esteem is the Self-Esteem Bucket. It is a simple activity that can be done on paper (you don't need an actual bucket.) I have also created a wooden puzzle with written prompts if you prefer (available on my website www.thetherapistparent.com).

The general concept is that we all have a self-esteem bucket. It represents our overall feelings about ourselves. What goes into our bucket are things that make us feel good about who we are. However, when negative things happen in our lives, they can cause holes in the bucket, and let some of our good feelings leak out.

Ask your child to think of positive situations and events in their life; encourage them to think of more than just their achievements. Ask what they think people like about them, e.g., their parents and friends. What makes them happy? Write these alongside a drawing of a bucket.

What will fill your bucket?
e.g.
- friends playing
- when I try and finally get it
- riding my bike
- playing the piano

Then explain that situations or events in life can make holes in the bucket, and the good feelings can leak out. These negative things can include other people's comments or reactions, your thoughts, or when things don't work out how you wanted. Have your child write a list of everything that puts holes in their bucket.

What puts holes in your bucket?

What will fill your bucket?
e.g.
- friends playing
- when I try and finally get it
- riding my bike
- playing the piano

@The_Therapist_Parent

Make sure you talk through any difficult feelings that arise as you do this part of the activity. Sometimes, children will raise an issue you had no idea would cause them to feel bad about themselves. It is important for you (and them) to realise what makes them feel bad so they can learn to do something about it.

The first part of this activity has helped the child see the positive and negative aspects of their life and how they contribute to their overall feelings of well-being. But we can't just leave their buckets with holes in them. That might make them feel hopeless. We need to encourage our children to find ways they can fix the holes and keep more of the positives inside.

What will fill your bucket?
e.g.
- friends playing
- when I try and finally get it
- riding my bike
- playing the piano

What puts holes in your bucket?
- people saying mean things
- I miss the ball
- I don't win
- can't do school work

What plugs the holes?
- hugs
- play with someone else
- remember I am a good at other things
- know I'm loved
- remember I do win sometimes

@The_Therapist_Parent

Explain that there are ways that we can help ourselves feel better when we spring a leak in our bucket. Talk to them about what they can do to feel better. They might be tempted to say, "Tell the teacher," if someone is mean. While this may be the right strategy for the situation, it doesn't really help with their feelings. Get them to come up with ideas that help remind them of good feelings in these situations, as well as what actions they can take.

Work with your child to identify plugs that fit the holes. In other words, guide them toward ideas that will help in the negative situations they have described.

Once you have all the information, it is important that the child makes this project their own. Let them get creative and have them colour and draw their thoughts, feelings, and ideas onto the page.

This activity helps children better understand the concept of self-esteem and allows them to see their strengths and difficulties. Identifying what they can do to plug the leaks in their bucket also empowers them with a plan to cope with their leaks.

Tree of Me Activity

It can be hard for kids to understand what their strengths are. When you ask them what is good about them they will usually say, "I'm nice" or, "I'm good at soccer." These are good, but we want kids to understand that there so many great things that make them who they are. That's how 'the Tree of Me' came about.

Start by drawing a bare tree. Make sure you draw the roots, too.

Talk about how our roots are our supports. These are the people who love us and that we can go to for help. Usually this will be family and teachers, but make sure you ask the child who they think their supports are. Talk about how these people help us. How when we go to them for help they will give us what we need. It can be advice, a hug, and safety. Write these on the roots.

Next we need to identify their strengths. Try to focus on their character traits, not their achievements yet. Draw them on the leaves. They can be things like, kind, try new things, never give up. If a child says, "I play games," you could reframe this as, "So, you are fun?" "Are you also a good friend?"

Next, you can write on their achievements. These are the fruit of their strengths. That's why I like to do them as apples. You can look at their strengths to work out their achievements. The strength 'I keep trying' would result in the fruit 'I ride my bike well.'

Writing this out is a good start. Having it drawn visually is helpful for kids to see just how many strengths and achievements they have. However doing this in one session can be difficult. It is hard to come up with everything on the spot. It can help for the child to ask family and friends what they like about them. Kids often don't realise that other people see positive things in them. By asking others, it also helps the child truly believe that they have these qualities.

If possible, it can be good to draw a big tree to put on their bedroom door. Make sure you have extra leaves and apples so that when you think of more you can add them.

Or, if a child has been working hard to achieve something, you can acknowledge this by adding it to the tree. In this way, the tree grows with them.

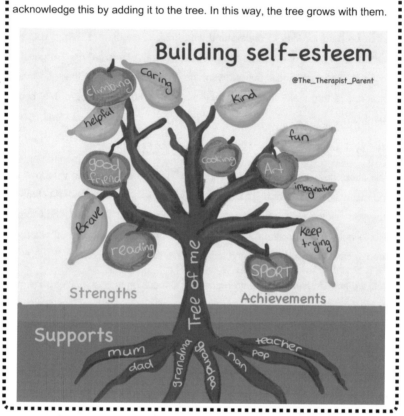

237

9.

Emotional

Intelligence

Building Emotional Intelligence

Many people struggle to understand the difference between intelligence and emotional intelligence. However, they are two completely different abilities. Someone can be incredibly intelligent and able to solve mathematical problems, but that doesn't mean they can problem-solve a solution when someone's feelings are hurt.

Research has shown that a person's emotional intelligence is a more significant indicator of success than their intellectual intelligence (Goleman, 2021). In other words, we should be far more concerned about how our kids perform in the playground than in the classroom.

So, What Is Emotional Intelligence?

Put simply, emotional intelligence is the ability to recognise emotions in yourself and others. It relates to how well you can regulate your own emotions and know how you can help someone else with what they feel (Goleman, 2021).

Four Key Areas of Emotional Intelligence

1. Self-Awareness

Recognising how we feel in a situation is an integral part of emotional intelligence. If we can't recognise our emotions, we become slaves to our reactive behaviour. When we can recognise our feelings, we can also start to understand the situations and events that trigger us and the impact our reactive emotions have.

The ability to know what your emotions are will direct your behaviour. For example, a child hears someone has been talking about them behind their back. They have the opportunity to recognise that they feel hurt and sad rather than just experiencing a wave of emotion clothed in anger. With this understanding, we can change our reactions significantly.

Self-awareness also encompasses an appreciation of our strengths and weaknesses. Understanding limitations is essential, as it allows us to know when to ask for help. Similarly, when we know our strengths, we know what we are capable of and how we can help others. Understanding this is a key to positive self-esteem, which is an extremely important aspect in how we value ourselves and how we let people treat us.

2. Managing Emotions

If we understand our emotions, we also understand the physical cues each emotion provides us and when we need to intervene before they escalate. Emotional awareness gives us insight into what we feel and what will happen if we allow those feelings to escalate. Understanding that we have choices regarding our emotions represents emotional maturity. Emotional regulation is a difficult skill to master and one that adults often struggle with, so actively teaching our kids these skills before they have formed habits with negative emotional consequences is vital.

Managing our emotions also comes with added insights we can use to guide our behaviour. For example, if we realise that being trustworthy and conscientious is more important than the emotional reaction we want to express in a heated moment, we will respond more maturely. We will appreciate that telling a lie might help us avoid something uncomfortable in the short term, but having people trust us is far more rewarding. However, remembering that being able to think ahead like this is something that comes with brain development, and not something children will be able to do without support. You can talk about these considerations afterwards, but not in a shameful way, it isn't a skill they have yet. You are just laying the foundation.

3. Empathy and Social Awareness

Empathy is more than just recognising what another person is feeling. Empathy is understanding someone else's perspective and actively taking an interest in their problem.

Well-developed empathy helps children to build a sense of security and stronger relationships with the other children and adults around them. It encourages tolerance and acceptance of others, which enhances friendships and good mental health. That is why building empathy needs to be an important focus when parenting our children. We need to gently help them see other's perspectives, which while they are young, they can't do alone.

4. Social Skills and Positive Relationships

Taking turns, losing in a game, actively listening in a conversation, using manners, and managing conflict effectively are critical social skills and form the bedrock of emotional intelligence. It is through these skills that positive relationships are built. I will go into more detail about these in the next few sections.

Building emotional intelligence is incredibly important for success in almost all areas of life. We can't expect children to naturally build their emotional intelligence, it is up to us to teach them. We need to help them build their emotional awareness in themselves and others. Giving them skills to manage these emotions by letting them experience all emotions and helping them calm through the emotion (co-regulation) will develop independence in emotional regulation. As we coach them through daily relationships, showing empathy, and positive social skills, we are helping them grow in emotional intelligence.

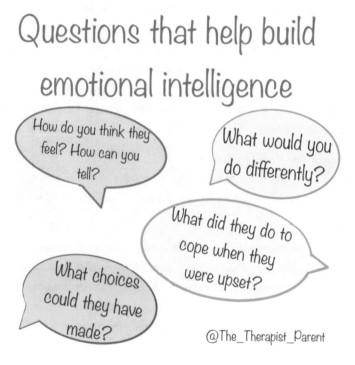

Feelings, Feelings, and More Feelings

If you have ever been to a psychologist, you've probably noticed that they talk about feelings A LOT. There is good reason for this obsession with recognising all the weird and wonderful emotions people have. When we understand what we are feeling, we give ourselves the opportunity to stop being reactive to our circumstances. Instead, we can choose an appropriate response. When we get caught up in an emotion, we go on autopilot, and our body/emotional brain takes over from our logical one. The purpose of this change of control is to keep us safe at any cost. If we can stop and label the feeling that caused the reaction, we often have the capacity to try and find a solution - and not feel so out of control.

Recognising emotions is also at the heart of emotional intelligence and is the key to interacting with people (see *Building Emotional Intelligence* on page 239 for more information). It is the ability to read what is happening within yourself and what those around you need. When you can do this, you regulate your emotions so they aren't out of control; you can also express them when needed. Reading emotions and sensing how other children respond to interactions allows your child to respond appropriately. This ability is the foundation for creating and maintaining friendships - an amazing skill to have, and one that starts with recognising feelings.

Labelling Feelings:

When kids are young, they can be overwhelmed with emotions that seem to crash over them like a wave. They have no control over the feelings, and don't really understand what they are. Our job is to label the emotion for them when we recognise it. Just like learning to speak, children need to learn the language of emotions. They need to connect the feeling of anger with their heart racing, getting hot, or wanting to yell and kick. When a feeling can be named, it becomes less scary, more normal, and something a child can recognise that others also experience.

There is scientific research that explains why labelling feelings is helpful. When we are in a highly emotional state, our limbic (or emotional) brain takes over. We can no longer think clearly and logically.

242

Our brain is in survival mode and will do what it needs to fight, flight or freeze. In this state, no amount of reasoning will change the way we feel. However, the research has found that if we can label the emotion, we will start activating the prefrontal cortex, or thinking part of the brain (Lieberman et al, 2007). Basically, when you or your child become overwhelmed by an emotion, simply being able to say what that emotion is will slow the emotional roller coaster. With this cascade slowed you can think more clearly to find a solution. Pretty impressive, really.

How to Teach Kids to Label Feelings

Draw the Body Cues

When kids are little, sticking to feelings such as happy, sad, angry, scared, and worried is fine. They are the building blocks for understanding emotions. However, as children get older, we need to expand their emotional vocabulary. For example, there is a difference between feeling angry and disappointed, or between confused and frustrated. How we would manage anger and disappointment will probably be different too.

One strategy that aids labelling feelings is for your child to draw what their body feels like while they are experiencing different emotions. You can talk about how some emotions have similar responses in our bodies. Being angry and being scared will both cause their heart to race, but they are very different emotions. It is important to help them see that while there are similarities, there are also differences they can look for.

If managing anger is difficult for your child, it can be helpful to work out what physical changes occur as their anger builds. Doing so will help them see the intensity of the emotion and can indicate when they need to stop before they become out of control. Their heart may race first; then they find themselves making a fist. This is followed by yelling, hitting, kicking, etc.

Some children can determine that if their muscles feel tight or they find themselves clenching their fist, they need to move away from the situation. Or, if they are anxious, they can use this method to see when they need to do controlled breathing, which will help relax their body. By helping kids understand what they are feeling, we provide them with insight into how to respond.

243

Be a Role Model

The best way for your kids to learn to label feelings and build an emotional vocabulary is to see you do it. Try to use specific words to describe how you feel. Rather than, "I feel good," you could say you are relaxed, pleased, or content. Recognise when you are frustrated and explain why. Try not to blame your child for your emotions, as we are all responsible for our own emotions. Don't say, "You are making me angry!" Try to say, "When I trip over the toys I have asked you to put away, I feel annoyed and frustrated." This description gives them a better idea of what these emotions look like and how they impact you. There is no better way to learn than in the moment. Or even better, when everyone is calm, talk about what happened together.

Use a lot of 'feelings language' at home in all sorts of situations. When your children are upset with each other, make sure you ask them both how they feel so they can each see what is happening for the other person. Learning about our emotions develops through watching others and recognising that what we do directly impacts how people around us feel. When you are watching TV together or reading a book, ask your child how they think the characters feel. Get them to consider if they have ever felt this way. Making emotions an everyday part of life will develop this understanding and encourage empathy for themselves and others.

Feelings Games

There are lots of games you can play that help build an understanding of emotions. You could play Charades, where you have to act out an emotion for another person. You could play Guess the Feelings Face, where you are given a drawing of a face feeling a particular emotion, and you have to describe situations that may cause you to feel that way. You can make this game harder by using a larger vocabulary of feelings. Basically, adding feelings to any game is going to help. If we can make feelings fun, then it will be easier for kids to learn.

Recognising and labelling emotions is an incredibly important skill. It physically changes our brain from being reactive to being more regulated and able to think logically in the face of emotional situations. It is also the foundation of emotional intelligence, something that will help our children succeed throughout life.

244

If we never let children go through the full wave of emotions,

when the emotion hits, there won't be the assurance that it will pass. That is scary

@The_Therapist_Parent

245

Feelings Activities

Feelings Games

Many games help build an understanding of emotions. You could play charades, where you have to act out the emotions. You could Guess the Feelings Face, where you are given a drawing of a face feeling a particular emotion and you have to describe situations that may cause you to feel that way. This can be made harder by using a large vocabulary of feelings words. Basically, adding feelings to any game will give your children practise and allow them to better understand the range of emotions they may encounter. If we can make feelings fun, then it will be easier for kids to learn.

Feelings Collage

For this activity, use old magazines and cut pictures from the magazines of people expressing any kind of feeling. Help them to use these images to build a 'feelings collage.' Try to have them elaborate on the details of what they noted regarding the person's facial expression, their body language, or the context of the photo or illustration that made them think the person in the picture was feeling the way they described.

Mirror Expressions

Mirrors are helpful for children to see how they look when they feel a certain way. It can help them understand what their feelings communicate to others. You can do this together and try to guess each other's feelings.

Jump on Feelings

Stick some drawings of feelings faces on the floor with some tape. Then call out the different feelings and the child jumps on that face. When they are on it, they need to say how their body feels when they have that emotion or they must think of a time when they felt that way.

Puppet Show

Put on a play with puppets. What actions may cause someone to feel sad or angry? Why might someone feel happy or excited about? Act it out.

Happy
relaxed muscles
smile
calm thoughts

Sad
heavy feeling
no energy
cry

Angry
heart beats fast
breathing fast
tight/strong muscles
want to hit/kick/yell
thoughts racing
hot

Scared/worried
heart beat fast, breathing fast
feeling in tummy
shaky body
want to run
thoughts racing

Emotional First Aid Kit Activity

Emotions can be very overwhelming. Anxiety, anger, excitement, worry, and embarrassment can all be difficult to manage, even for adults. As adults, we learn ways to manage our emotions, although we are not always good at it. We probably have a friend that we call if something goes wrong, make ourselves a cup of tea/coffee if we need to clear our heads, go for a run, or do something active if we are angry or anxious. We may not do this consciously, but we do have 'go to' ways to manage our emotions. Kids need these, too, but it is important to find what works for them. Putting ideas all together in a 'first aid kit' helps children to see that they have options and that they have a choice with how they can manage their emotions.

You can get crafty and make a kit as elaborate as you like. I have had clients who have bought beautiful special boxes, or painted shoe boxes. Have fun with it and make something that your child will love. But it really doesn't have to be anything too fancy. When I have made them quickly in my office, I have simply used A4 paper, a red felt-tipped pen and staples.

Brainstorm ideas with your child of things that help them feel calm. Try to think of things that are Relaxing, Distracting, Physical, and Social.

Relaxing

These are activities that help the body and mind calm. There are ideas about controlled breathing techniques, progressive muscle relaxation and visualisations in the section on *Mindfulness Activities* (page 191) that you could use. These are important to use when your child is beginning to become anxious or angry. When their heart rate is just starting to accelerate and they are becoming agitated. Relaxation activities are great at catching the feeling and stopping it from escalating. However, if they are already out of control, then relaxation activities might not be as effective and you might need to try some more physical activities.

If you see your child becoming anxious or angry, you can coach them through what they are feeling. For example, "You look like you are starting to get angry/worried." "Your muscles look tight and your face looks..." "Let's get something out of your first aid kit to help you feel better."

Relaxation ideas:

- Controlled breathing, paper boat, pinwheel.
- Glitter jar.
- Blow bubbles.
- Listen to music.
- Visualisations: have a photo of a favourite holiday, place, or time. Help them imagine what it looks, tastes, smells, feels and sounds like.
- Colouring.
- Painting.
- Squeezing play dough.
- Write in a diary.

Distraction

There is a place for distraction. I am all for children recognising their emotions and working through them, but sometimes they can get stuck in the emotions and distraction just shifts their thinking. Try to avoid screen time for this. Watching TV or video games can make children more agitated. Distraction activities are fun and completely different to the thing that has triggered the emotion. If possible, it is good to change the environment too. This will depend on your child. Some kids would happily play a board game while others would throw the board game across the room.

You just need to talk to your child ahead of time and see what they think will work. You might even need to decide this for your child, by giving them a job to do. A strategy that can be used in schools when a teacher sees that a child is starting to escalate, is to send them to the office to deliver a note. The note can say, "Please just send .... back to class." In the same way, if you see that your child needs distracting, you could ask them to help you with a job, go get the mail, etc.

Distraction ideas:

- Play a game.
- Look through photo albums.
- Cook.
- Write a story.
- Make a craft.
- Build a fort.
- Read.

Physical

If emotions like anxiety or anger have built up to the point that your child's heart rate has increased, their breathing is fast, or their muscles are tight, then relaxation and distraction are probably not going to work well. They will need to do something physical to release the fight/flight response that their body has prepared for. Physical activity will help the muscles and the breathing use up the the energy and come back to a calm state.

Physical ideas

- Kick a ball.
- Jump on the trampoline.
- Ride a bike or scooter.
- Punch a pillow.
- Run or go for a walk.
- Climb a tree.
- Go on a swing.

Social

We all need to know that we aren't alone. We need to know that other people are there and understand how we feel. It is important to identify with your child, ahead of time, who they can talk to and get help from. Have ideas for home and at school. Sometimes, kids need reminding that they can have help to manage emotions, and it is important to ask.

Social ideas

- Ask for help.
- Have a hug.
- Talk to someone you trust.
- Visit a friend.

Once you have come up with ideas from each category, write them down on paper and have your child draw a visual reminder next to each one. Fill your first aid kit with as many ideas as you can. It is important for your child to see that they do have options.

Have the first aid kit somewhere that is easy to get, and see. Maybe on the fridge or in their room. If they are feeling like they need help to calm, encourage them to take something out of the kit. They do not have to do the first thing they pull out. If they pull out 'jump on the trampoline,' and it is raining, they can just choose another one. They can keep choosing until they find one that they think will help.

Make sure you praise your child for choosing to do something to help manage their emotions. Even if they do it a bit late. If they become very angry, yelled, etc. but then use their kit to calm down, acknowledge that they did something you are proud of. You may, at some stage, talk to them about trying to catch the emotion a bit earlier, but it is still positive that they have used it.

Emotional First Aid Kit for kids

Physical Activity

Social needs

FIRST AID

Distraction

Relaxation

@The_Therapist_Parent

Emotional Vocabulary Activity

We often hear about how we should help children build an emotional vocabulary, but why?

It's important for children to develop an emotional vocabulary because it assists in making them aware of what is happening in and around them. It provides the language to describe their feelings and clues to what needs to happen.

Feelings are there for a reason. Just as pain is a protective factor that keeps us safe and prevents further harm. Feelings let us know what is happening within and around us and point to what we need to do to make a situation right. If you touch something hot, you pull away to stop getting burned. When you get annoyed, it might mean that someone has crossed a boundary. The earlier we recognise these signs in our bodies as feelings that need to be expressed, the better we become at accurately identifying them. We then build our ability to manage the feelings as they increase in intensity. As a result, we also learn to generate empathy for others.

Verbally expressing emotions can be difficult for anyone, but it is even more difficult for children. Given a child's underdeveloped vocabulary, they may not have the words to describe the difference between being frustrated and annoyed, or being scared and nervous. However, they can point to a chart that visually represents this. We can create a visual chart that incorporates the language around emotions. This helps children understand the difference between feelings of annoyance, upset, frustration, anger, and furiousness. If we link these with physical cues, we can also teach about the intensity of an emotion.

Visual scales are useful to help children recognise and describe the emotional stages they experience, develop emotional intelligence, and empower them to see that they have choices around managing their own emotions. When making a visual scale, make sure you involve your child in creating something they like and can relate to. Place it somewhere that can be easily seen, and make sure you talk about it often, not, for instance, just when they are feeling angry.

Using paint charts (as pictured on following page) is a great way to show the varying intensity of emotions. We don't just experience being happy, sad, angry, and scared. There are so many other shades of emotions, such as relaxed, cheerful, unhappy, miserable, irritated, furious, concerned, nervous, or terrified. How we manage all these emotions varies, and we need to explore what we can do to feel better. Children need to learn that feelings are normal, they change, and there are things we can do to help.

If you can identify the different levels of emotion with your child, have them talk about how they feel differently. How do they know when they are disappointed or frustrated? What's the difference? What are the clues in their body that can help them work out the intensity of the emotion? Brainstorm with your child actions they can take at the varying stages of intensity that could help them feel calmer. Write them on to your visual chart so that the child can see that there are solutions to help with emotions when they arise. This allows them to realise that they aren't helpless; they can manage their own feelings.

The ideas that you use to help calm your child will vary depending on what setting you are focusing on. What the child can do at school will be different from what they can do at home. However, the key is to come up with as many ideas as possible. Be creative; if they feel like throwing things, what can they safely throw, and where would this best be done? Scrunched-up paper is safe and quite satisfying, although they may need to clean it up once they are calm. There is a big difference between feeling concerned and terrified. Once a child has become terrified, there is not much they can do other than get help from a parent or someone they trust. However, if they are concerned, they can recognise that something is wrong and talk to someone. They could do some controlled breathing or move away from what is making them feel uncomfortable. Children need to become aware of options for every level of intensity. This way, they learn that many different paths exist, and they can find the ones that work best for them given their situation.

By increasing a child's understanding of emotions in themselves and others, they will be better equipped to cope with those emotions constructively. When we build our emotional vocabulary, we build our resilience and emotional self-management.

Next time someone asks how you are doing, instead of simply responding with, "Okay" or, "Fine," try practising your emotional intelligence by using more emotionally accurate words. Remember, the best way to teach our children an emotional vocabulary is to model it ourselves.

Developing Empathy and Its Importance

When we think about what we want our kids to be like, we usually say things like, "I want them to be kind, thoughtful, and helpful," among other things. We want them to think about others and do good in the world. None of this is possible if our kids don't develop empathy. Not only does empathy impact who they will be and what they will do in the future, it also affects the relationships and friendships they will have throughout their lives.

It is challenging to function socially with peers if you lack insight into how others feel. If someone has underdeveloped empathy, they won't know how to communicate with the people around them. They won't understand if what they are saying is what the other person wants to hear or if they are upset by it.

Empathy is more than just understanding how someone is feeling. There are three distinct processes involved in empathy (Decety and Cowell, 2014):

1. Emotional Sharing: When we feel similar emotions in response to observing someone else. We connect with the person's feeling and know what that feels like.

2. Empathetic Concern: Which is the motivation to care for someone who is distressed. When we understand how someone feels and we want to help.

3. Perspective-taking: The ability to imagine how the other person feels. To really put yourself in someone else's 'shoes.'

We can't expect that children will be able to do all three of these processes.

Empathy is a complex skill. Having empathy requires us to see ourselves as separate from someone else. It means we understand that other people have different thoughts and feelings. However, before we can show empathy, we need to recognise and understand common feelings, such as when we or others are happy, sad, angry, or scared. On top of this knowledge, we need to be able to imagine how a person may feel in different situations and have some insight into what we could do to help. When we consider it, that is a lot to know!

256

There is some research to suggest that children begin to have an understanding of other people's feelings from about two years of age (Abedon, 2005). But the ability to put yourself in someone else's shoes is not fully developed until about five–seven years of age.

Developing empathy doesn't just happen the way a child gets their first tooth. Some things need to be in place to develop empathy. Such factors include having a safe, connected relationship with a caregiver. Still, there are things that we can do to help improve empathy.

We Have to Model Empathy

Kids are more likely to learn empathy if they experience it. We need to ensure that when our kids are experiencing big emotions, we don't shut them down or dismiss them as silly. We need to help our kids learn what their feelings mean; they will need us to label the emotions for them, especially when they are young. The more we say things like, "I understand that you are worried" or, "I can see that you are angry," the more we help our children connect with their bodies and the emotions they experience. This modelling also helps them become better at reading feelings in themselves and others. When we engage in this way, we also validate their emotions so they realise that someone understands how they feel. Then, when an offer of help is made, we can navigate the emotions with them and let them feel compassion.

You can also explain how you are feeling in different situations. Just be careful not to make your children feel responsible for your feelings. If you say, "You make me sad when you do that," you directly connect them to your feelings. Instead, say, "When my vase got broken, I felt sad." Connect the behaviour to the feeling rather than the child. That way, they realise they need to change that behaviour, not themselves.

Look for Opportunities

Always look for opportunities to help build empathy. It doesn't matter if it is watching a TV show, reading a book, or seeing people interact in the park. Talk to your child about the emotions and perspectives of others. "How do you think they felt when that happened?" "What do you think they were thinking?" "How would you feel?" "What would you do in the same situation?" This can also be done in a structured way, through role-playing and games that encourage 'mind-reading.'

Conflict between siblings is the perfect opportunity to build empathy. Try not to compete in a screaming match, that won't help anyone. When the situation is calmer, try to get the children to see how they each felt. If one child was hurt, have the other look at their facial expression and body to connect with the emotion. Once they have acknowledged how the other felt, then they have to work out, together (with your help), what they can do to help each other feel better. Now, if one child had just bitten another, the hurt child may not want a hug, and saying sorry may not be enough. We want our kids to understand the impact of their behaviour, not just rattle off a "Sorry." It might be a letter, to play a game, or share a toy, but it has to be something they both agree with.

Don't Desensitise

People don't really like to think about the impact of violent video games or television programs, but the research is clear: Being exposed to violence makes people less empathetic (Brockmyer, 2022). It was found that exposure to violent media, especially violent video games, can cause desensitisation to real-life violence. Desensitisation to violence blocks empathy, which is needed to trigger the moral reasoning process that triggers prosocial responding. This decrease in empathy is not only from violent video games, though. You just have to watch the news to be exposed to the horrible things people are capable of. I strongly suggest not letting young children watch or hear the news on TV or the radio. It seems that in every news bulletin, there are shootings or acts of violence. Ultimately, this exposure can desensitise us and can lower our empathy toward others.

There is plenty you can do, however, to employ empathy at home and help your child develop a strong sense of it. If they experience, see, and practice empathy, they will develop into the kind, caring, and helpful people we hope they will grow up to be.

If children are going
to develop empathy,
they need to see,
experience and
practice empathy

@The_Therapist_Parent

Empathy-Building Games

Empathy X-ray

I was inspired with this activity from Kristina Marcelli (www.kristinamarcelli.worpress.com). it is a great way for children to really understand how someone feels on the inside. It shows the impact of their behaviour but also shows that on the inside, we are all the same. The fact that someone is showing that they are angry, may be the result of their feelings being hurt, something that can't always be seen on the outside.

This activity helps children notice how they feel in certain situations, and especially when they show empathy and compassion to others.

- First, ask the child if they know what an x-ray is and explain that it shows what is inside our body.
- Ask the child to draw the x-ray scan for what it feels like inside their body when they help and show kindness to others. Even very young children can identify the response in their bodies to engaging in compassionate behaviours towards others.
- Encourage the child to notice these sensations when they make compassionate choices in the future to further encourage and reinforce compassion and empathy.

To make this activity even more playful and fun, include puppets! Act out social situations and have the child pretend to take an x-ray of the puppet after positive and negative interactions with others.

Empathy Game

This game not only helps children recognise other people's feelings but also what they can do in these situations. You can use any tray or container, but a muffin tray works well. Write people that the child knows down and put a name in each muffin hole. Then use some coins, balls, beanbags, whatever you have, and write or draw feelings on them.

Have the child throw a feeling into the muffin tray. Now get them to describe a time they saw that person feel that way. You can then build on this by brainstorming what they can do when this happens.

But remember, you can have all the tips and tricks, but you need to be practicing empathy at home if you are going to help your child develop a strong sense of empathy themselves.

Emotional Intelligence - Social skills

Children are often referred to me for 'social skills training.' But what does that even mean?

In general, social skills are how we communicate and interact with others, verbally and non-verbally. It involves knowing when and how to talk to someone, as well as understanding 'social rules' and when to follow them. Developing social skills is a vast topic with many components, involving what we do with our bodies, how we communicate verbally, appreciating social expectations, and using manners.

To master social skills, we need to know how to manage the following things:

Physical behaviour
- Eye contact (or if eye contact is problematic, turning their head toward the person),
- Tone and volume of voice,
- Body language, and
- How close we stand to other people.

Verbal Behaviour
- How to have a reciprocal conversation,
- How to engage in small talk, and
- How to ask to play.

Social Rules
- What to do when you lose,
- How to take turns,
- How to share equitably,
- What to do when someone smiles at you,
- Which things you can do in public and private,
- How to manage conflict, and
- What to do if someone gives you a present you don't like.

262

Manners

- Knowing when to say thank you,
- How to greet people,
- How to say goodbye, and
- Saying please.

There is far too much on this topic to tackle in one article. For now, let's focus on how social skills relate to Emotional Intelligence.

When we look at social skills in terms of emotional intelligence, the main focus is on how we make and maintain friendships. With children, this is incredibly important. Every day, they are in a highly social environment (e.g., at school), and there is no way to avoid people and play. The impact of not being able to negotiate this world successfully affects the child's self-esteem, which will, in turn, impact their ability to learn. While some kids will naturally be better at this, it is not something that just happens. Social skills are learned, and we need to give our kids opportunities to develop these.

Developing Social Skills

Start with the Basics

When we meet people, we usually look at them, smile and, often, say hello. It is not enough to tell children to do this. We need to explain why it is necessary. When these skills make sense to a child, they are more likely to do them. When we look at people, we give them our attention, letting them know we are listening.

Children who are Autistic or have a language disorder can find eye contact difficult. Basically, reading the cues from someone's face, as well as processing the information they are saying at the same time, is too demanding. In such situations, it is acceptable to look towards a person but take breaks by looking away for short periods. Another option is looking at the person's forehead rather than in their eyes. I am not suggesting you force an Autistic child to make eye contact, as that could cause incredible stress. Having options other than direct eye contact can make it easier for these children, especially when they are in situations where others don't understand this difficulty. As not everyone understands the full scope of neurodiversity, having a few tricks can help reduce social pressures.

Social smiling is another form of communication. We smile at people so that they feel comfortable. It is a way of saying "Hello" and/or letting others know it is okay to talk to them. Sometimes, we need to explicitly explain this to children. Role-playing or using puppets can be helpful when teaching these skills. Have children practise what it feels like when they try to talk, and the person (or puppet) doesn't look at them or in their direction. Ask your child, "What does it feel like if you walk up to someone and they frown at you? Would you want to play with them?"

Most young children don't realise they need to greet people to start an interaction. Often, they will try to join a game without saying anything or, alternatively, hide on the periphery in silence and wonder why they are not included. We must explain that we usually start with a "Hello" or other greeting when we meet someone or see them for the first time that day. Just as you would start a sentence with a capital letter or the alphabet with an A, you start an interaction with a greeting.

Playing Games

Playing games sounds simple, but there is more to it than we might first think. How many times, as parents, have we had to step in when a game turned into a yelling match? Playing a game can be difficult. It involves turn-taking, understanding how the other is feeling, and the ability to respond well when things don't go your way.

While playing, it is important to teach children that they should focus on more than the end goal of winning. It is also favourable to take an interest in the other player/s; offering encouragement or helping others in the game helps to build friendships. Be sure to talk to your child about what to do when they lose. It can help to remind them before a game starts that losing is okay. Also, let them know that it's more fun to play and lose than not play at all, and no one can win every time, but they might win the next game.

The only way to build these skills is to practise them, and having an adult coach them when issues arise can be invaluable. If there are siblings, then great. That is the perfect place to start. However, if your child is an only child, you will have to be their playmate. Ensure you talk them through these skills, and don't just let them win every time.

Managing Conflict

Conflict is bound to happen. It is part of all relationships, but managing it well is a fundamental skill for life. Of course, how your child manages conflict will depend on their age, but it is never too early to start teaching them the best ways. In this instance, we need to start with what not to do. Children must be made aware that hitting, punching, kicking, or hurting someone they conflict with is unacceptable. It is also not helpful to yell or call each other names, throw things, or wreck the game for everyone else. We don't do these things because it damages friendships. It is crucial to get away from the 'you're not my friend anymore' way of thinking and teach them that they can disagree with someone yet still be friends. However, it is not enough just to tell your child what not to do; you have to give them a plan they can carry out when conflict occurs.

When conflict does occur, the first thing a child needs to recognise is when they are starting to feel angry or upset. If you need more guidance on how to help your child identify this, there are some ideas in the article titled *Building Emotional Intelligence* on page 239. When children can observe these cues, they can then take appropriate action.

Young children (preschool-aged) will need help with this skill. We must teach them that when they get angry or upset in a game, or the other child does, they can get help from an adult. It is then the adult's job to coach them through what to do. Remember to listen to their feelings empathetically and label the emotions that are displayed, e.g., "You didn't win the game. That is really hard. Sometimes I get angry when I don't win too." Offer comfort to help them calm down and then problem-solve together what they could do next. A child might need a hug and support to calm themselves, or they may like to try again. Some children will need time to do something alone before they are ready to interact again. Be sure to talk to them about how the other child may feel, too, without causing shame. They must learn to see situations from other people's perspectives, but they are not responsible for others' feelings. You could ask, "How do you think the other child is feeling right now?" rather than, "You are upsetting the other child."

With older children (school-aged), the process is similar. The only difference is that we want them to follow the process more independently if they are able. However,

265

it is important that even though these children are older, they still know they can ask for help if they need it. Again, role-play and practise are great ways to build these skills.

It can be tempting as a parent to ban a game if conflict regularly results. However, if children can negotiate this, they have the opportunity to develop fundamental life skills. If a board or other game causes conflict, it is okay to have a break, but try to have your kids return to it after they have resolved the problem.

Social skills related to emotional intelligence are vital for children, especially when placed in highly social environments such as preschool and school. Learning to greet, play games, and manage conflict will directly impact their ability to make and maintain friendships. To make these challenging skills a little easier, we must intentionally coach them through everyday situations.

Personal Space Activity

Having a good understanding of personal space helps everyone feel more comfortable in social situations. It also gives way to teaching that consent is needed to be in someone else's personal space.

Explain that we all have an invisible bubble around us called our personal space. You can show the size as being roughly an arms length away. So put your hand on their shoulder and keep your arm outstretched, this is a general rule for keeping personal space.

Explain why having personal space is important. You can demonstrate this or role-play it. If you stand too far away from someone, they may not think you are interested or they may not hear you. If you stand too close or touch someone, they may feel uncomfortable.

Act out what personal space looks like in different scenarios. The rules for this will be different depending on the relationship. This is a good opportunity to discuss space and touch for different people in their lives. This can be extended to include the types of conversations that are appropriate for different people as well.

To work on specific social rules for different relationships, you need to show this clearly. Draw a circle and write the child's name in the middle. Draw circles around this, as many as needed. In the first circle, write all the people that are closest to the child. This is usually mum, dad, siblings but there could be others. The next circle usually includes extended family and close family friends. The next, includes friends, the next might be teachers or other trusted adults. It is a good idea to add police and other helpful adults. The last circle will have people we meet, shop assistants, etc.

It is helpful to colour code the levels so you can make quick and easy reference to what the social rules are. For example when in a shop, you could remind your child that the shop assistant is in a blue zone, which would mean no hugs, just smile and say, "Hello."

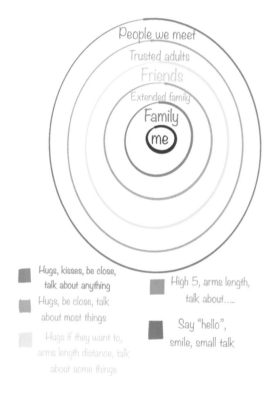

Hugs, kisses, be close, talk about anything

Hugs, be close, talk about most things

Hugs if they want to, arms length distance, talk about some things

High 5, arms length, talk about.....

Say "hello", smile, small talk

Write what the rules are for each zone next to the circles.

You can adjust this to any social skill that you need to work on. It could be how we greet people who have different relationships with us. Or, there could be topics that your child has been talking about that are not appropriate for someone they have just met. You can add rules to the zones. You can also discuss how someone could be in a zone, but as the relationship changes their zone will change. It is adaptable to what you need.

Voice Activities

We say a lot without really speaking. Our volume, tone of voice, and body language speak volumes. Children don't always understand this. They think that if they grunt, "Sorry," then they have said the right thing. Or, if they whine, "OKAYYYYYYY" when they are asked to do something, that we should just be happy they are doing it. While we may have some tolerance for this at home, our children need to understand that there are rules around this form of language. The issue with this is more when it happens in the playground, classroom, or other social environment. It will impact their friendships (or ability to make friends), how they are viewed by adults, and generally thought of by the people around them. Just like learning to speak, we need to learn the language of volume, tone, and body language.

Volume

How many times do you have to say, "You are speaking too loudly" or, "Use your inside voice"? It can be hard to understand why there are different volumes for different places. We need to speak quietly in a library, but we can yell in a park. We try not to speak too loud in a restaurant, but we can sing happy birthday, loudly, in the same restaurant. Children tend to respond best to visual explanations. Too many words can just be overwhelming and confusing. When it comes to helping kids to understand volume, I find using a 'volume meter' works the best.

Draw a simple meter with a scale of 1-10. Draw an arrow and attach it with a split pin. That way you can move it across the scale.

Have fun with your child, practising what each volume sounds like. 1 is very quiet, you can hardly hear it. 10 is so loud that the neighbours across the street could hear you. 5 is usually a normal speaking voice. Brainstorm with your child where it would be okay to use these different volumes. A 2 might be when you are at the movies and they need to tell you that they need to go to the toilet. Have them think about what might happen if they asked using volume 10. You might use an 8 to call out, "Coming ready or not!" in a game of hide and seek, so that everyone knows that you are coming. If you only used a 2, people wouldn't know that they had to hide and they may get angry. In working out these scenarios, children can understand why we have rules and how their volume impacts others.

Once you have the numbers and volumes well established, it can make discussions around volume so much easier. Instead of, "Inside voice," you can say, "Volume 5." When you are going somewhere where the expectation is to be quiet, you can explain this easily. For example, "When we are in the church for the wedding, your volume needs to be at 2. Once the service is over, it can be a 5." Often, kids may not realise that their volume has escalated, especially if they are excited. If this happens, you simply say, "You are at an 8, you need to be a 5."

Tone of Voice

The meaning of a sentence can change dramatically based on what tone we use. We can effectively convey a feeling simply by the tone, even if the words don't match. The meaning can also change depending on which words you emphasise in the sentence.

Sometimes, kids don't even realise when they are changing the meaning of the sentence by saying things in a certain way. Here is an example using one simple sentence.

"I love doing homework today."

Try reading this out loud like you are excited. Now try worried. And angry. It is amazing how the same sentence can take on different meanings just based on the emotions you use when talking.

Another example of how the meaning can change is by emphasising different words. Have a go with your child. Try emphasising the word "I" in the sentence above. Next try emphasising "love," "homework," and "today." The sentence will mean different things when you emphasise different words.

When Reading: When you are reading with your children, pick out a sentence or two, and see how the meaning of the sentence changes when you emphasise different words or use different emotions

When Watching a Show: Point out when a character's tone of voice or emphasis on a particular word changes the meaning of a sentence.

Fun With Sentences: Try practising the sentences below with your children, using different feelings, or emphasising different words, or both.

Some examples:

- "I love ice cream."
- "I'm going to the library."
- "Do you want to play?"
- "I have sport today."
- "I have to catch the bus today."

Body Language Activities

Children need to understand that body language is important. Just like words can hurt someone's feelings, body language can do the same thing. When you roll your eyes or turn your back and walk away, it says, just as if you had shouted it, that you don't care and don't respect the person. You can use body language to let others know that you like them and care for them, without ever having to say a word. Just like if you were to hug me or hold my hand, I could tell you loved me without having to say it. Here are some games to build this awareness.

Guessing Games

Show your child how different body movements can convey clear and specific emotions. Tap your fingers, shrug your shoulders, fidget, and stand with your hands on your hips. Explain the unspoken message behind each movement. "When someone is standing like this, it can mean that they're losing patience. Or, they're upset by what you're saying."

Silent TV

You can bring the concept of body language to life by noticing how people—both in real life and on TV—are interacting. (If you're watching TV together, you can even turn the sound off.) Help your child spot clues that indicate how each person is feeling. Ask what clues made you think that the person felt that way. Saying things like, "The man's face was looking down" or, "The girl's fists were clenched," gives your child a way to remember the visual cue.

Play Body-Language Charades

Acting out emotions through body language helps kids see the connection between the two. Make a game of it. On cards, write different emotions (one per card). These could include happy, sad, angry, tired, and so on. Take turns picking up a card and acting out the emotion while the rest of the group tries to guess what it is.

Teaching Problem-Solving

Whether it is conflict resolution, managing emotions, or creativity in general, problem-solving is the skill that underpins success in them all. Research shows that children who learn problem-solving skills will improve their mental health and be less likely to suffer from depression as adults (Maddoux et al, 2014). These are pretty good reasons to help our kids learn to problem-solve.

Children who do not develop problem-solving skills tend to avoid challenging situations. They won't grow in confidence and independence through achieving something difficult. And they may also respond impulsively rather than working through an issue. Often, the child experiences even more problems as their impulsivity gives them no time to think about the consequences of their actions. On the other hand, children who do develop these skills can manage their emotions, think creatively, and persist through challenges until they find a solution.

Obviously, our expectations of a child's problem-solving ability will depend on their stage of development. We wouldn't expect a two-year-old to be able to think of several alternatives to a problem and determine which one is more likely to be successful. But we can start introducing problem-solving skills from around three years of age. These skills can be taught through incidental play and guided opportunities. It is our job as parents not to jump in and solve every difficulty for them but to teach them how to work through a problem for themselves.

Children Under Five Years Old

The first stage of problem-solving is recognising and managing emotions. You can't expect a child to think through a situation if they are overwhelmed by emotions. The thinking part of the brain will literally not be able to function when a child is in the midst of all-consuming emotions. It is our job to 'emotion coach' them through. They can't do this for themselves. It is a skill that they have to learn.

1. Firstly, we name their feeling for them. By doing this, we help them understand what is happening and what their emotions are. This also validates the child's emotion, so that they feel understood. You can say, "I can see you are really disappointed that we can't go to the park." This gives them language for the feelings that have overtaken them.

272

2. Then, connect with your child and help them to calm. There are strategies you can use in the articles titled *Co-regulation With Children of All Ages* on page 46 and *Mindfulness for Children* on page 188. But basically, you will need to support your child to become calm before you can offer any ideas to solve their problem. Hug them, sit with them, and just wait until the wave of emotions settles. It will pass, and sometimes you just need to wait it out before you can move on.

3. When everyone is calm, you can support your child's problem-solving. You can brainstorm what they could try the next time they have the same issue. See if they can come up with some ideas. Let them guide your suggestions. If they are still upset, add some silly ideas like, "Could we go to a park on the moon?" They will see that this is not possible, and it will encourage them to come up with some alternative ideas.

Try asking your child, "What isn't working?" if they are frustrated by something they can't do. This can help them see the problem from a different perspective. Once this is worked out, you can come up with solutions together.

<u>**Five years and above**</u>

Children that are a little older can have more independence with problem-solving. They may still need help to go through the process, but they should be able to work through the stages themselves. It can be helpful to link the five steps below to each finger on their hand.

1. What am I feeling? As you would with younger children, older children may still need help to recognise their feelings. Provide labels for the emotions if they need them. If they understand that they are sad, rather than angry, they may not respond as impulsively. Knowing what you are feeling gives you clues as to what you can do

2. What is the problem? Help them see what the problem really is. What is their role in the situation? Try to help them to see the situation from every perspective.

3. What is the solution? Have them come up with as many ideas as possible to solve their current issue. Any possibility, 'good' or 'bad,' should be explored. For example, if they are angry at someone, they could punch them. That is a possibility. It is not a 'good' option, but it doesn't hurt for them to think through what would happen if they did take such an action.

4.What could happen? Next, encourage them to think through each idea. What would happen if they tried each? Which one do they feel is best?

5. Choose one. Have them try their idea. Remember, if it doesn't work, they can try one of their other options.

Problem-solving is an important skill to learn

3. Possible solutions
4. What would happen?
2. What is the problem?
5. Choose the best
1. How do I feel?

@The_Therapist_Parent

What Parents Can Do

Model Problem-Solving

When you are faced with a problem that is appropriate for your child, think aloud about it. Model how you would solve it. Work through the stages with them listening.

Ask Them What They Think

Ask your child what they think you should do. This allows them to practise problem-solving skills, but it also helps them feel valued.

Don't Give Them the Answers

As tempting as it might be to just tell children what they need to do, try to let them solve their own problems. You can guide them and offer suggestions, but as much as possible, try to get them to think of what to do.

Let Them Experience Natural Consequences

When appropriate (and not dangerous), let your child make their decision and experience the consequences, such as choosing not to wear a jacket and experiencing the cold. Later, you can talk about what they would do next time they faced a similar decision.

We need to remember that problem-solving doesn't just happen by chance. It is a skill that is learned through experience. We must be careful that our good intention to fix their problems doesn't rob our children of the knowledge they need to build these skills. We are here to coach them so that they can be independent, confident, and creative problem-solvers.

If we want children to learn to problem solve, we have to step back.

Try asking

"what isn't working?"

"Which bits are hard?"

"What can you do?"

@The_Therapist_Parent

Problem-Solving Activities

Puzzles: Puzzles are great for developing thinking skills. The puzzle is literally a problem to solve. Rather than putting a piece in for them, ask, "Could you put it a different way?" Guide them, but let them work it out.

Blocks: Everything your child builds will have challenges. They need to think through their design and construction and find a way for it to be stable. If their tower doesn't work, avoid diving in and fixing it. Ask them, "Why do you think it didn't work? What else could you do?"

Memory Games: Memory games help build focus and attention; skills needed to think through a problem and solve it.

Story Time: Make the most of a book to help develop problem-solving skills. While reading a story, pause and ask your child questions. Ask, "What do you think they should do?" "What else could they have done?" Have them see that there are always many options to solve a problem, but some will work better than others.

Role-Play: While adults often dislike role-plays, children tend to love them. It is a fantastic way for children to practise problem-solving. They get to play out what would happen in a given situation and can try many options without consequence. Come up with real or imagined scenarios and have children brainstorm what to do, acting out what would happen.

Creative Play: The best lessons are learned through play. Give your child unstructured activities to do. Suggest they build a fort, a cubby house, make a plane with Lego, etc. Come up with creative options and then stand back and let them work out how to do it.

Board Games: Games that encourage strategy and forward-thinking are great for problem-solving. Monopoly, or similar games, work well. Just be sure to choose games that are not won by chance.

Break the Problem Down: As children get older, the problems they tackle can be more complicated. Include scenarios that have multiple aspects that could be contributing to the problem. For instance, your child could be late for school every day. Get them to think through all the possible causes. For example, they might be tired from staying up too late, have slept through the alarm, haven't packed their bag, and/or are trying to finish their homework because they didn't do it the day before. Once you've helped them identify each factor, let them devise strategic solutions to solve the issues. Encourage them to realise that one solution may solve more than one problem.

Reference List

Abedon, E. (2005). Toddler Empathy: Awareness of people's feelings may start at a young age. https://www.parents.com/toddlers-preschoolers/development/behavioral/toddler-empathy/

Alloway TP, McCallum F, Alloway RG, Hoicka E. (2015) Liar, liar, working memory on fire: Investigating the role of working memory in childhood verbal deception. Journal of Experimental Child Psychology 137:30-8.

Attwood, T. Evans C. & Lesko A. (2014). Been There. Done That. Try This!: An Aspie's Guide to Life on Earth. London: Jessica Kingsley Publishers.

Bamford, C. and Lagattuta K. (2011). Looking on the Bright Side: Children's Knowledge About the Benefits of Positive Versus Negative Thinking. Child Development 83(2): 667-682.

Brockmyer, J. (2022). Desensitization and Violent Video Games: Mechanisms and Evidence. Child and Adolescent Psychiatric Clinics of North America. 31(1):121-132.

Brummelman E, Thomaes S, Orobio de Castro B, Overbeek G, Bushman BJ. 2014. "That's not just beautiful—that's incredibly beautiful!": the adverse impact of inflated praise on children with low self-esteem. Psychol Sci. 25(3):728-35.

Buysse, D., Grunstein, R, Hornec, J. & Lavie, P. (2010). Can an improvement in sleep positively impact on health? Sleep Medicine Reviews, 14(6) 405-410.

Couglan, S. (2016). Safer Internet Day: Young ignore 'social media age limit' https://www.bbc.com/news/education-35524429.

Cross, D.S., & Walker, J. (2015). Using research to inform cyberbullying prevention and intervention. In S. Bauman, D.S. Cross & J. Walker (Eds), Principles of cyberbullying research: Definition, methods and measures (pp. 274-294). Routledge.

Dawkins, R. (2018). The Importance of Sleep for Kids. https://www.hopkinsallchildrens.org/ACH-News/General-News/The-importance-of-sleep-for-kids.

Decety, J. & Cowell, J. (2014). The complex relation between morality and empathy. Trends in Cognitive Science 18(7):337-9.

Emmons, R. & McCullough, M (2004). The Psychology of Gratitude. Oxford University Press, USA.

Fields, D. (2016). Why We Snap: Understanding the Rage Circuit in Your Brain. Dutton.

Flook, L., Smalley, S., Kitil, M.J., Galla, B., Kaiser-Greenland, S., and Locke, J. (2010). Effects of Mindful Awareness Practices on Executive Functions in Elementary School Children. Journal of Applied School Psychology 26(1) 70-95.

Gasper, K. & Middlewood, B. (2014). Approaching novel thoughts: Understanding why elation and boredom promote associative thought more than distress and relaxation. Journal of Experimental Social Psychology. 52. 50-57.

Gleason, M., Boothe, A. (2020) Managing Behavioral Issues in Child Care and Schools. A Quick Reference Guide. American Academy of Pediatrics.

Goleman, D. (2021). Emotional Intelligence: Why it can Matter More than IQ. London, Bloomsbury.

Goodwin, Kristy (2021) Raising Your Child in a Digital World. Homeschooling Global Summit, YouTube.

Gottman, J. (1997). Raising an Emotionally Intelligent Child. Simon & Schuster.

Green, A., Cohan-Zion, M., Haim, A. & Dagan, Y. (2017). Evening light exposure to computer screens disrupts human sleep, biological rhythms, and attention abilities. The Journal of Biological and Medical Rhythm Research 34(7): 855-865.

Henderlong J and Lepper MR. (2002). The effects of praise on children's intrinsic motivation: A review and synthesis. Psychological Bulletin 128(5): 774-795.

Hölzel BK, Carmody J, Vangel M,(2011). Mindfulness practice leads to increases in regional brain gray matter density. Psychiatry Res.;191(1):36-43.

Kennedy-Morre, E, (2013). Chores and Children - Getting kids to help with housework. Psychology Today. https://www.psychologytoday.com/us/blog/growing-friendships/201303/chores-and-children.

Lapointe, V. (2019). Parenting Right From The Start: Laying a Healthy Foundation in the Baby and Toddler Years. Vancouver: Life Tree Media.

Leonard, E. (2018) How To Raise A Secure Child, Parenting With Empathy Dr Erin Leonard; 1st edition (March 17, 2018).

Lieberman, E., Michel, J., Jackson, J., Tang, T. & Nowak, M. (2007). Quantifying the evolutionary dynamics of language. Nature volume 449, pages713–716.

Maddoux, J., Symes, L., McFarlane, J., Koci, A., Gilroy, H. & Fredland, N. (2014). Problem-Solving and Mental Health Outcomes of Women and Children in the Wake of Intimate Partner Violence. Journal of Environmental and Public Health. Article ID 708198, 7 pages, 2014. https://doi.org/10.1155/2014/708198.

Mahoney, S. (2014). The 7 Reasons Your Kid Needs Sleep. https://www.parents.com/health/healthy-happy-kids/the-7-reasons-your-kid-needs-sleep.

Markham, L. (2012) Peaceful Parent, Happy Kids: How To Stop Yelling and Start Connecting. Penguin publishing.

Mikolajczak, M, James J. Gross, Roskam I, (2019). Parental burnout: What is it, and why does it matter? Clinical Psychological Science 7(6): 1319-1329.

Mizokawa, A. (2018). Association Between Children's Theory of Mind and Responses to Insincere Praise Following Failure. Frontiers in Psychology.

Mueller CM and Dweck CS. 1998. Praise for intelligence can undermine children's motivation and performance. Journal for Personality and Social Psychology 75(1): 33-52.

Napoli, M. (2004). Mindfulness Training for Teachers: A Pilot Program. Journal of Evidence-Based Integrative Medicine 9(1).

Nelson, J. (1985). The Three R's of Logical Consequences, the Three R's of Punishment, and the Six Steps for Winning Children Over. Individual Psychology: Journal of Adlerian Theory, Research & Practice, 41(2), 161-165.

Owens, J.A., Dearth-Wesley, T., Lewin, D., Gioia, G., & Whitaker, R. (2016). Self-regulation and Sleep Duration, Sleepiness, and Chronotype in Adolescents. Pediatrics. 138(6), https:doi.org/10.1542/peds.2016-1406

Richardson, H. (2013). Children should be allowed to get bored, expert says. https://www.bbc.com/news/education-21895704

Scott, A, Webb, Martyn-St James, M. Rowse ,G and Weich S. (2021). Improving sleep quality leads to better mental health: A meta-analysis of randomised controlled trials, Sleep Medical Review. 60: 101556

Siegel, Daniel, (2001). The Developing Mind: How Relationships and the Brain Interact to Shape Who We Are. Guilford Publications.

Stanton R, Rosenbaum S, Kalucy M et al. 2014, 'A call to action: exercise as treatment for patients with mental illness', Australian Journal of Primary Health, 21(2) 120–125.

Whiddon, M. A., & Montgomery, M. J. (2011). Is touch beyond infancy important for children's mental health? Retrieved from http://counselingoutfitters.com/vistas /vistas11/Article_88.pdf.

Zhang, D., Chan, S., Ming Lo, H., Chan, C., Chan, J., Ting, K., Gao, T., Lai, K., Bögels, M. & Wong, S. (2017). Mindfulness-Based Intervention for Chinese Children with ADHD and Their Parents: A Pilot Mixed-Method Study. Mindfulness 8: 859–872.

Zhou, Z., Qing-Qi, N, Geng-Feng,S. Xiao-Jun, F., Cui-Ying (2016). Bullying victimization and depression in Chinese children: A moderated mediation model of resilience and mindfulness. Personality and Individual Differences, 104, 137–142.

Made in the USA
Columbia, SC
16 June 2024

37210835R00163